....

PUPPY'S NAME

....

BIRTHDAY

Acadia Goldendoodles

BIRTHPLACE

....

FIRST DAY AT HOME

Need extra help or a more personalized approach? Our professional trainers will guide you alongside this self-paced program - answering questions, sharing expert advice, and reviewing assignments to keep both you and your puppy on track! Contact us at **www.biscuittraining.com** for more information.

Copyright © 2020 by Joanna Russell

All rights reserved. No part of this publication may be reproduced, distributed, or transmitted in any form or by any means, including photocopying, recording, or other electronic or mechanical methods, without the prior written permission of the publisher, except in the case of brief quotations embodied in critical reviews and certain other noncommercial uses permitted by copyright law. For permission requests, write to the publisher, addressed "Attention: Permissions Coordinator," at the address below.

ISBN 978-0-578-71963-4

Printed in the United States of America
First Edition, 2020
Cover Design by Tatiana Pavlova

Biscuit Training
San Francisco, CA

www.biscuittraining.com

DISCLAIMER

This program provides general information about puppy training and raising for dogs 8-20 weeks of age. The author makes no representations or warranties about the accuracy, applicability or completeness of information in this program, and assumes no liability for any consequences, loss, or damage caused or alleged to be caused by the information in this program.

CONTENTS

HOW TO USE THE PUPPY TRAINING AND RAISING PROGRAM 9
WHAT TO KNOW ABOUT THE SECTIONS IN EACH WEEK 12
LEARNING OUTCOMES 14

PREPARING FOR YOUR PUPPY 17
PUPPY PARENTING 101 20
GETTING READY 22
FOOD 28
DESIGNING A DAILY ROUTINE 30
SETTING UP YOUR HOME 34
PARENTING DECISIONS 38
DANGEROUS FOODS 42
CHECKING VITAL SIGNS 44

FIRST MONTH AT A GLANCE 51

WEEK ONE: WELCOME HOME 55
WEEK ONE CURRICULUM 58
FIRST VETERINARIAN APPOINTMENT 62
SOCIALIZATION 66
FIELD TRIPS 72
HOUSETRAINING 74
APARTMENT HOUSETRAINING 78
CRATE TRAINING 82
BARKING AND WHINING 88
PLAY-BITING 92

ISOLATION DISTRESS	94
NAME RECOGNITION	98
MARK THE MOMENT	100
CORRECTIVE FEEDBACK	104
GAMES: "FOLLOW THE LEADER" & "SEEK"	106
WEEK TWO: GETTING TO KNOW EACH OTHER	**109**
WEEK TWO CURRICULUM	112
BASIC OBEDIENCE TRAINING TIPS	116
LURING AND VERBAL CUES	118
PUPPY COMMUNICATION	120
LEASH TRAINING	122
RESOURCE GUARDING	124
LURED SIT	126
LURED DOWN	128
RECALL	132
WEEK THREE: SETTLING IN	**137**
WEEK THREE CURRICULUM	140
JUMPING UP	144
STAY	146
TOUCH	148
GAMES: "CATCH ME IF YOU CAN" & "FETCH"	150
WEEK FOUR: MANNERS PLEASE	**153**
WEEK FOUR CURRICULUM	156
SIT	160

DOWN.. 162

SECOND MONTH AT A GLANCE... **165**

WEEK FIVE: NOT EVEN THE DRYWALL IS SAFE..................................... **169**
WEEK FIVE CURRICULUM... 172
CHEWING... 176
LEAVE IT... 178
DROP IT.. 180
GAMES: "TUG-OF-WAR" & "RED LIGHT, GREEN LIGHT" 182

WEEK SIX: GOOD HABITS LEAD TO BETTER RESULTS........................ **187**
WEEK SIX CURRICULUM.. 190

WEEK SEVEN: PROOFING MAKES PERFECT.. **195**
WEEK SEVEN CURRICULUM... 198
PROOFING.. 202
EVALUATING BEHAVIORS.. 206
GAMES: "HIDE AND GO SEEK" & "GUESS WHO"............................. 208

WEEK EIGHT: THEY GROW UP SO FAST... **211**
WEEK EIGHT CURRICULUM.. 214
LOOSE LEASH WALKING.. 218
NAME REDIRECTION.. 222
PUPPY REPORT CARD... 224

EXTRAS.. **229**

HOW TO USE THE PUPPY TRAINING AND RAISING PROGRAM

❧ INTRODUCTION ❧

Welcome to puppy ownership! You have embarked on a rewarding experience that will bring you happiness for many years to come. This program will teach you everything you need to know to help your puppy grow and develop into the well-behaved best friend you've always wanted.

The interactions you have with your puppy will shape the kind of dog your puppy will soon become. How you live and interact with your puppy around the house is the greatest predictor of whether or not it will grow up to be a well-adjusted and well-behaved dog. This puppy training and raising program was designed to ensure that your puppy gets the proper foundation needed to become the companion you will not only love, but also love to live with. The focus each week will be on teachable moments that matter, building good habits into your puppy's daily routine, socialization, and basic obedience.

HOW THE PROGRAM WORKS

Think of this less as a book and more as a step-by-step interactive weekly guide to help you train and raise your new puppy. The content is paced to match the developmental milestones of your puppy, and focus on the most important information you need to know, when you need to know it. This approach keeps things simple and manageable, never overwhelming you with needless details or distractions.

Each week, you'll find an outline of the key tasks to accomplish over the next seven days, along with learning outcomes to expect. The curriculum also includes helpful information about why to include specific activities into your daily routine, and the importance of teaching specific behaviors. Read the week's information prior to starting the week and use the checklists to keep track of your progress. If at the end of the week you feel that your puppy isn't not ready to move on to the next week's material, it's best to repeat the content for another week until your puppy can master the objectives. There are checklists throughout the program to keep track of progress.

WHAT TO KNOW ABOUT THE SECTIONS IN EACH WEEK

Developing Good Daily Habits

Your puppy is always learning - behind their every action is a curiosity and desire for your feedback. This section highlights ways to interact with your puppy, giving you simple routines to incorporate consistently to make sure your puppy is learning right from wrong and avoiding preventable behavioral issues.

10-Minute Training Sessions

Basic obedience behaviors play an important role in raising a well-behaved puppy. Each day of the week you will be given specific behaviors to teach your puppy, using a 10-minute morning and afternoon training session. Getting your puppy to a) understand and b) reliably perform behaviors under different circumstances and in different environments requires a lot of repetition and practice! To account for this, the program allottes plenty of time to practice behaviors with your puppy over multiple training sessions and weeks.

Socialization

The socialization checklist will walk you through 10 different experiences to introduce or expose your puppy to. If you are comfortable taking your puppy on field trips, they are an efficient way to check experiences off the list. Everyone's life circumstances and situations are different, so if you find a socialization experience that isn't relevant to where you live and your lifestyle, feel free to skip it. The important thing to keep in mind with socialization is whether or not you can reasonably expect your puppy to have a similar experience down the road (e.g. if you don't have kids now but plan to start a family one day, you'll want to socialize your puppy with kids). If your dog's breed is genetically predisposed to having stronger protective instincts or to being sensitive and timid, be sure to put a strong emphasis on socialization.

Field Trips

Field trip suggestions are provided to aid in thoroughly and efficiently socializing your puppy. These activities can play an important part of your puppy's socialization routine.

NOTES

LEARNING OUTCOMES

This Program Provides a Foundation for Preventing Some of the Most Common Behavioral Issues:

- Isolation Distress and/or Separation Anxiety
- Ongoing Housetraining Issues
- Crate Avoidance
- Biting and Chewing
- Jumping
- Demand Barking
- Resource Guarding

- People Aggression
- Dog Aggression
- Anxiety and Reactivity Towards New Stimuli
- Fear of the Outdoors
- Sound and Surface Sensitivity
- Handling Difficulty
- Leash Pulling

And Provides a Foundation for the Following Behaviors:

- Sit
- Down
- Touch
- Loose Leash Walking

- Stay
- Recall
- Drop It
- Leave It

GOALS

MONTH 1

- [ ] Socialize — peoples, animals, environments, daily life
- [ ] Come, greeting manners, Stay, alone time/crate training
- [ ] Leave it/look, leash walking, training w/ distractions

MONTH 2

- [ ] Leash walking
- [ ]
- [ ]

WEEKLY GOALS

- [ ]
- [ ]
- [ ]
- [ ]
- [ ]
- [ ]
- [ ]
- [ ]

PUPPY TRAINING AND RAISING

PREPARING FOR YOUR PUPPY

❖ INTRODUCTION ❖

WHAT TO KNOW: PREPARING FOR YOUR PUPPY

Preparing for life with a puppy will make the transition to becoming a puppy parent not only easier and less stressful, but also a whole lot more enjoyable! Whether you've already brought your puppy home or you're expecting your puppy in the near future, it's never too late to make a few thoughtful preparations.

SECTIONS TO READ	DONE
Puppy Parent 101	☐
Getting Ready	☐
Food	☐
Designing a Daily Routine	☐
Setting Up Your Home	☐
Parenting Decisions	☐
Dangerous Food	☐
Checking Vital Signs	☐

PRIORITIES

- [ ]
- [ ]
- [ ]
- [ ]
- [ ]
- [ ]
- [ ]
- [ ]

TO-DO LIST

- [ ] Design daily routine
- [ ] Field trip - drive thru
- [ ] Field trip - breweries
- [ ] Field trip - beach
- [ ] Field trip - skate park/ prom
- [ ]
- [ ]
- [ ]

PUPPY PARENTING 101

WHAT YOUR PUPPY NEEDS

New puppy parents are great at providing their puppy with lots of love and affection. There is no doubt that puppies need affection, but by focusing your attention on predictability, consistency, and confidence, you'll be well on your way to raising a well-behaved and happy puppy.

Structured, Predictable Daily Routines

Puppies, like children, love structure and predictability in their lives. The ability to anticipate what's next in the daily routine provides them with a sense of security and comfort, while setting the stage for them to quickly learn how to behave at home. For example, you'll notice that as your puppy gets used to set nap times throughout the day, they will naturally start becoming more calm as their next nap approaches.

Consistent Feedback

Your puppy needs consistent and binary feedback: what they are doing correctly and what they are doing incorrectly. Each interaction with your puppy is a teachable moment and if your lessons are 100% consistent, your puppy will have no trouble understanding what you want and how they should be behaving.

Calm, Confident Puppy Parent

Every puppy needs a calm confident puppy parent that provides clear behavioral guidance and leadership on a daily basis. Your puppy will not only be more comfortable, but also much happier when they follow your lead. All you have to do is show them the way!

NOTES

GETTING READY

MY PUPPY COMES HOME ON:

These handy checklists will help make sure you don't miss any of the important preparations for your puppy's arrival. Many of these items will be discussed in more detail later in the section, so don't worry if you're not ready to check the box!

TO-DO LIST

- [ ] Decide on your puppy's daily routine
- [ ] Ask your breeder and/or rescue organization what brand of food they are currently feeding your puppy
- [ ] Buy supplies
- [ ] Set up your puppy's crate(s)
- [ ] Set up your puppy's exercise pen and/or puppy room if you are planning to have one
- [ ] Puppy proof your home
- [ ] Register for puppy socialization classes
- [ ] Schedule your puppy's first veterinarian appointment
- [ ] Schedule pet sitters for your first week back at work
- [ ] Consider pet insurance
- [ ] Notify your home insurance company that you're adding a dog to your policy
- [ ] Apply for a city pet license
- [ ] Invite family or close friends to visit at the end of the first week your puppy will be home
- [ ] Prepare a first aid kit for your puppy

PUPPY PROOFING

- Secure any trash containers out of your puppy's reach ☐
- Manage and conceal loose wires and cords ☐
- Store medications and supplements in a secure area ☐
- Check if any of your houseplants are poisonous for dogs (many are) and remove, where appropriate ☐
- Store household cleaning products in a secure area ☐
- Keep battery powered devices out of reach ☐
- Look around your home for items that might look "chewable" and store, where appropriate ☐

PUPPY FIRST AID CHECKLIST

Vaccinations and Medical Records	☐	Collapsible Food and Water Bowls	☐
Hydrogen Peroxide	☐	Towel or Blanket	☐
Antibiotic Ointment	☐	Food	☐
Gauze (made for animals)	☐	Water	☐
Scissors	☐	Treats	☐
Tape	☐	Medications	☐
Rubber Gloves	☐	Extra Leash and Collar	☐
Wet or Grooming Wipes	☐	Poop Bags	☐

SUPPLIES

- [ ] Crate(s)
- [ ] Crate bed insert
- [ ] Dog bed
- [ ] Exercise pen and/or baby gates
- [ ] Food and water bowls
- [ ] Food
- [ ] Training treats
- [ ] Training treat pouch
- [ ] 4-6-foot leash
- [ ] 30-foot long-line leash
- [ ] Front Attaching Harness
- [ ] Flat collar
- [ ] Brush and shampoo
- [ ] Nail clippers or nail dremel
- [ ] Dog toothbrush and toothpaste
- [ ] Active Playtime toy(s)
- [ ] Chew toy(s)
- [ ] Puzzle and interactive food dispensing toys
- [ ] Pet ID tag
- [ ] Pooper scooper and poop bags
- [ ] Pee pads, training turf and/or grass (if you plan on starting housetraining indoors)
- [ ] Enzyme cleaner

The Pros and Cons of the 5 Main Types of Crates

CRATE TYPE	PROS	CONS
Metal Wire Crates	• Good for dogs that need to see their surroundings to settle down and relax • Well ventilated for hotter climates • Can be fitted with removable divider panels • Collapsible	• Some dogs find the lack of privacy stressful • Noisy • Easier to escape from
Plastic Crates	• Good for dogs that are easily distracted or feel anxious about their surroundings • Light, portable, and easy to clean • Good for car rides and airline approved	• Some dogs prefer more visibility and may find it stressful • Reduced ventilation
Soft-Sided Crates	• Extremely light and portable • Easy to store • Washable • Easy to set up in hotels and/or campgrounds	• Not suitable for destructive dogs or escape artists • Difficult to keep clean between washes • Better for more experienced dogs • Not ideal for crate training or anxious dogs
Heavy Duty Metal Crates	• Very durable—can contain the most destructive dogs or talented escape artists • Safest option for car rides	• Expensive • Not the most attractive • Better for more experienced dogs who have already been crate trained
Stylish Crates	• More easily blends into the home decor • Wide variety of styles to choose from	• Poorly suited to destructive dogs • Any accidents may leave stains and odors • Typically more expensive

HELPFUL TIPS

- 🐾 A crate that is too big for your puppy will increase the likelihood that they will use one end as a bathroom. Your puppy's crate should be just big enough for them to stand up, turn around, and lie back down.

- 🐾 It's a good idea to get a resizable crate or a crate with a divider so that you can continue to use the same crate as your puppy grows.

- 🐾 A retractable leash is not recommended because it teaches your puppy to pull on the leash.

CRATES

What Size of Crate Does My Puppy Need?

CRATE SIZE	DOG WEIGHT	BREED EXAMPLE
18"-22" (45-56 cm)	Extra Small	1-10 lbs	Yorkshire Terrier	Chihuahua
24" (64 cm)	Small	11-25 lbs	Pug	Bichon
30" (76 cm)	Medium	26-40 lbs	French Bulldog	Cocker Spaniel
36" (91 cm)	Intermediate	41-70 lbs	Basset Hound	Australian Cattle Dog
42" (107 cm)	Large	71-90 lbs	Golden Retriever	Labrador
48" (122 cm)	Extra Large	91-110 lbs	Akita	Doberman Pinscher
54" (137 cm)	Giant	Over 110 lbs	Great Dane	Irish Wolfhound

NOTES

SUPPLIES BUDGET

SUPPLY EXPENSE   BUDGET   ACTUAL

TOTALS
DIFFERENCE

FOOD

HOW TO FEED YOUR PUPPY

ALWAYS START WITH THE SAME FOOD YOUR BREEDER HAS BEEN USING: Slowly phasing out any food your puppy has already become accustomed to will reduce the chance of developing an upset stomach.

SMALL QUANTITIES, FREQUENTLY: Ration food out evenly throughout the day. As a rule of thumb, puppies need four meals a day until they are twelve weeks old, three meals a day until they are six months old, and two meals a day thereafter. Larger breeds may cut the number of meals from three to two sooner than 6 months.

INVEST IN QUALITY FOOD FORMULATED FOR PUPPIES: Puppies grow 20 times faster than adult dogs and require specially formulated food to support their rapid physical development.

DON'T OVERFEED: Growing too quickly or getting too fat can create other concerning health issues for your puppy.

NO FOOD BEFORE BED: Feeding your puppy right before bed will likely lead to a midnight bathroom break.

AVOID SUDDEN CHANGES : Sudden dietary changes can really upset your puppy's tummy. Slowly introduce any new food over the course of several meals.

NO EATING BEFORE CAR RIDES: Feeding your puppy right before a car ride encourages motion sickness.

NO TABLE FOOD WHILE YOU'RE EATING: If your puppy never tastes human food they won't beg or drool while you're having a snack or sitting at the dinner table. Ignorance is bliss!

HELPFUL TIPS

- Some medium and large-size breeds are susceptible to a serious medical condition called bloat. Seek advice from your breeder or veterinarian on what precautionary measures you can take when feeding your dog in order to avoid this condition.

- You will go through a lot of treats when teaching your puppy new behaviors. A trick to avoid overfeeding - using some of the kibble from their next meal during training sessions in lieu of treats.

KONG KIBBLE STUFFING RECIPE

Throughout the puppy training and raising program you will be asked to use chew toys stuffed with treats; here is one recipe to get you started!

INGREDIENTS

1 cup puppy kibble

1 cup water

Scoop of peanut butter (xylitol free)

DIRECTIONS

1. Add one cup of water to a cup of your puppy's kibble
2. Let the kibble sit and soak up the water
3. Fill the Kong ¾ of the way full with the kibble mixture
4. Add a scoop of peanut butter to fill the Kong

- To relieve your puppy's sore gums while they are teething or to make the Kong treat last longer, freeze the Kong treat overnight. Naturally, frozen Kongs are more difficult to eat so make sure your puppy has experience with Kong treats before freezing it, or they may lose interest.

- Wash the Kong in the dishwasher after your puppy is finished

DESIGNING A
❖ DAILY ROUTINE ❖

WHY YOUR PUPPY NEEDS A DAILY ROUTINE

One of the most important things you can do for your puppy is structure, and follow, a predictable daily routine. New dog owners have a tendency to start off with too little structure in the early days of puppy ownership, and find themselves having to add more structure when behavioral problems inevitably develop. As your puppy matures, you will gradually give them more freedom when they prove they can handle it responsibly. Until then, your puppy will appreciate a structured routine - it will teach them how to behave and helps them fit in with their new family.

Page 32 has an example of a well-planned daily routine for a new puppy. Use this as a guideline, then create your own daily routine in the blank table that follows.

HOW TO DESIGN A DAILY ROUTINE

- Work in enough potty breaks. Plan to give your puppy 10 or more opportunities a day to go potty in their designated potty area.

- Enforce naps. Puppies need between 16-18 hours of sleep a day and should be awake for no more than two consecutive hours.

- Be strategic about how you use your puppy's daily allotment of kibble. Don't give them all of it in a bowl.

- Plan out your puppy's awake time activities in advance (see next page).

AWAKE TIME ACTIVITIES

ACTIVE PLAYTIME: Fetch, tug-of-war, and keep away are just a few of the many games you can build into your routine. Keep biting to a minimum by having toys close by to redirect your puppy's needle sharp teeth.

SELF-DIRECTED PLAYTIME: Interactive food dispensing toys and puzzles are a great way to keep your puppy entertained when you're not around to supervise.

CHEWING AND LICKING: Bully sticks, dog bones, and lick mats are the equivalent of giving your puppy a soother. These will help when you're looking to lower your puppy's energy level.

SOCIALIZATION: There's always someone new to meet or something new to see! Expose your puppy to the world around them!

TRAINING: Teaching your puppy is one of the best ways to drain their batteries. Puppies love to learn!

GROOMING: Grooming sessions are most successful when your puppy is tired, so plan accordingly. And don't forget about good dental hygiene!

EXERCISE: Once vaccinated, off-leash or loose-leash walks are a great way to exercise a young puppy.

CUDDLING: One of the best parts about having a new puppy in the family!

HOW TO INTEGRATE KIBBLE INTO YOUR DAY

- 🐾 Put it in interactive toys and puzzles.
- 🐾 Use it as a reward during training sessions.
- 🐾 Give it to your puppy during socialization activities.
- 🐾 Keep a supply on hand at all times to reinforce your puppy's good behaviors in the moment.

DAILY ROUTINE EXAMPLE

TIME	BATHROOM BREAK	ACTIVITY
7:00 AM	🐾	*Training Session, Breakfast*
7:30 AM	🐾	*Playtime*
8:00 AM		*Chewing & Licking*
8:30 AM	🐾	*Naptime*
9:00 AM		
9:30 AM		
10:00 AM		
10:30 AM	🐾	*Exercise*
11:00 AM		*Snack, Playtime*
11:30 AM	🐾	*Naptime*
12:00 PM		
12:30 PM		
1:00 PM		
1:30 PM	🐾	*Snack, Playtime*
2:00 PM	🐾	*Self Directed Playtime*
2:30 PM		*Chewing & Licking*
3:00 PM	🐾	*Naptime*
3:30 PM		
4:00 PM		
4:30 PM		
5:00 PM	🐾	*Training Session*
5:30 PM		*Socialization, Exercise*
6:00 PM		*Self Directed Playtime, Dinner*
6:30 PM	🐾	*Chewing & Licking*
7:00 PM	🐾	*Naptime*
7:30 PM		
8:00 PM	🐾	*Playtime*
8:30 PM		*Chewing & Licking*
9:00 PM	🐾	*Grooming*
9:30 PM		*Cuddling*
10:00 PM	🐾	*Bedtime*
2:30 AM		

PUPPY TRAINING AND RAISING

YOUR DAILY ROUTINE

TIME	BATHROOM BREAK		ACTIVITY
7:00 AM			
7:30 AM	✓	potty	Breakfast, Playtime (20 min)
8:00 AM			Training Session (~~10~~ 3 min)
8:30 AM			Tether time (20 min)
9:00 AM	✓	potty	Naptime in crate
9:30 AM			
10:00 AM			
10:30 AM	✓	potty	Exercise (recall practice)
11:00 AM			
11:30 AM			Snack/lunch
12:00 PM			
12:30 PM			
1:00 PM			
1:30 PM			
2:00 PM			
2:30 PM			
3:00 PM			
3:30 PM			
4:00 PM			
4:30 PM			
5:00 PM			
5:30 PM			
6:00 PM			
6:30 PM			
7:00 PM			
7:30 PM			
8:00 PM			
8:30 PM			
9:00 PM			
9:30 PM			
10:00 PM			
2:30 AM			

SETTING UP YOUR HOME

WHY YOUR HOME SETUP IS IMPORTANT

A good home setup paired with a structured and predictable daily routine is often the difference between a happy and easy transition to puppy parenthood and a challenging exhausting one. Being thoughtful about how you are setting up your home can minimize your puppy's homesickness, keep them safe when unsupervised, reduce whining and crying, and lower the number of bathroom-related accidents in your home.

DAYTIME SETUP

Crate setup should be in an area of your home where your puppy won't feel isolated from the rest of the family; this is known as the "area of inclusion". You can either use the same crate you have in your bedroom (see night setup below) and move it during the day or invest in a second crate. If you decide to buy two crates, consider a plastic crate for your bedroom and a wire crate for your area of inclusion. Plastic crates have less visibility which means less visual stimulus for your puppy when they need to rest; the wire crate does the opposite, making your puppy feel more included.

Crate your puppy during the day when they can't be supervised and/or when you want them to enjoy some awake time alone. If you want your puppy to have more space to move around when you can't supervise them, you can either cordone them off in an exercise pen (temporary playpen made of metal fencing) or a puppy-proof room. If you take either of these approaches, leave their open crate inside this space so they can freely go in and out.

When your puppy naps, place them in their crate in your bedroom. If you don't have two crates and prefer not to move the crate back to your bedroom for nap time, that's ok as long as your puppy is able to settle down and go to sleep. If you have a wire crate and your puppy is having trouble settling down and going to sleep, drape a lightweight blanket over the top of the crate to reduce the number of distractions in the surrounding environment (making sure to leave enough of the wire crate uncovered for airflow).

NIGHT SETUP

Your puppy should spend the night sleeping on something comfortable and chew-proof in their crate (close to your bed, if possible). A crate is not only the safest place for your puppy to sleep at night, but also having it close by makes it easier when you need to get up in the middle of the night for a late night bathroom break. Puppies have no need for pyjamas, so avoid any type of night time sleep wear. Finally, make sure you close the crate door securely once they are inside.

DAYTIME SETUP FOR WORKING PUPPY PARENTS

If you can't be with your puppy during the day, and don't plan on having someone come to let your puppy out of their crate, it's best to keep your puppy in an exercise pen or puppy-proof room. Ensure that they have access to their crate, pee pads or training turf (at a corner furthest away from their bed), water, food and a chew toy stuffed with treats.

Puppies are very social animals and crave companionship, and have a hard time being alone for a full workday. If at all possible, have someone come to your house once or twice a day to let your puppy out to engage and interact with them while you are away.

HELPFUL TIPS

- It's good for your puppy to have open access to their crate all day. You'll find that they'll wander there because it gives them a sense of security while providing a cozy, private, resting area.

- Having your puppy sleep in your room can reduce the amount of whining and crying that are driven by isolation distress. It also keeps you tuned into requests to be let out in the middle of the night for a bathroom break. Once your puppy drops the night time pee break, you can move their crate to another room in the house if you prefer.

NOTES

DESIGN YOUR PUPPY ROOM

PARENTING 🐾 DECISIONS 🐾

INADEQUATE SOCIALIZATION VS INFECTIOUS DESEASES

Puppies typically come home between 8-12 weeks of age and, during this time, two important things are going on in their lives. First, they begin receiving vaccinations for critical communicable diseases like parvovirus and, second, they enter an important socialization period where formative development milestones occur. Unfortunately, these two areas of your puppy's life are in direct conflict with one another. A puppy is not fully protected from infectious diseases until approximately 16 weeks when they complete a series of vaccinations. Some veterinarians, appropriately concerned about the risk of exposure to unvaccinated dogs, recommend keeping puppies at home until then. The counterargument is that puppies who follow this advice will completely miss an important socialization window which ends around the 14 week mark. Puppies who are forced indoors will not become familiar with the details of everyday life and are far more likely to develop significant, and potentially lifelong, behavioral issues.

WHAT SHOULD YOU DO?

You will receive a lot of advice on the topic from educated pet professionals but, at the end of the day, it comes down to a tradeoff between different risks. Remember that the choice is yours! To help inform your decision, here are a few more key points to be aware of:

- The American Veterinary Society of Animal Behavior's official position is that *"the primary and most important time for puppy socialization is the first three months of life. During this time puppies should be exposed to as many new people, animals, stimuli and environments as can be achieved safely and without causing overstimulation manifested as excessive fear, withdrawal or avoidance behavior. For this reason, the American Veterinary Society of Animal Behavior believes that it should be the standard of care for puppies to receive such socialization before they are fully vaccinated."* They add that, *"in general, puppies can start puppy socialization classes as early as 7-8 weeks of age. Puppies should receive a minimum of one set of vaccines at least 7 days prior to the first class and a first deworming. They should be kept up-to-date on vaccines throughout the class."*

- Behavioral problems are the greatest threat to the owner-dog bond and are the number one cause of relinquishment to shelters. Behavioral issues, not infectious diseases, are the number one cause of death for dogs under three. Appropriate socialization during critical periods of puppy development, particularly up until 16 weeks, helps reduce behavioral problems.

- Parvovirus is highly contagious and spreads from dog-to-dog by direct or indirect contact with their feces. There is evidence to suggest that the virus can live for up to a year in soil. Mortality can reach 91% in untreated cases and treatment often involves extensive stays in veterinary hospitals. A combination of maternal immunity, primary vaccination, appropriate care, and precautions can minimize the risk of infection to puppies who are brought outside.

HELPFUL TIPS

- If you decide that you want to keep your puppy at home, try bringing as much of the outside world into your home as possible. Have people over to meet your puppy; the more diverse the group, the better. If those guests have puppies and/or dogs of their own who are up-to-date on their vaccinations, invite them along too. Flip through the weekly curriculums in this program and review the socialization checklists. With a bit of creativity, you can still complete a lot of the recommended activities.

- If you decide to bring your puppy outside, minimize their risk of infection by taking additional precautions. Carry your puppy to and from your car and keep them in your lap, or in a carrier, cart or stroller. Don't bring your puppy to high traffic areas for dogs such as dog parks or popular walking paths. Don't let any dogs that you don't know interact with your puppy, period. Ensure that any puppy socialization class you sign up for strictly enforces its vaccination policy and provides a clean environment for your puppy. Finally, take your puppy on lots of car rides; they can see and hear a lot of the world from the safety of your car!

NOTES

PUPPY PARTY PLANNING

Whether you decide to take your puppy outside or keep all your socialization activities indoors, hosting a puppy party is a good idea. Here is a handy party planning list to get you started:

DATE | LOCATION

_____

GUESTS	Y	N
	☐	☐
	☐	☐
	☐	☐
	☐	☐
	☐	☐
	☐	☐
	☐	☐
	☐	☐
	☐	☐
	☐	☐
	☐	☐
	☐	☐
	☐	☐
	☐	☐
	☐	☐
	☐	☐

❖ DANGEROUS FOODS ❖

DANGEROUS FOODS FOR PUPPIES AND/OR DOGS	WHAT CAN HAPPEN
Xylitol (found in gum, candy, etc.)	Liver Failure | Hypoglycemia | Death
Avocados	Vomiting | Diarrhea
Alcohol	Coma | Death | Intoxication
Onions and excessive amounts of garlic	Blood Cell Damage | Anemia
Caffeine	Vomiting | Diarrhea | Toxic to the Heart and Nervous System
Grapes	Kidney Failure
Raisins / Currants	Kidney Failure
Dairy products	Diarrhea
Macadamia Nuts / Walnuts	Nervous System | Muscle Damage
Chocolate	Death | Toxic to the Heart and Nervous System
Cooked bones	Stomach Lacerations
Mushrooms (some varieties)	Shock Death
Human medications	Kidney Failure | GI Ulcers | Death
Fatty foods	Pancreatitis

HELPFUL TIPS

🐾 Keep hydrogen peroxide in your home in case your puppy eats something toxic and your vet recommends inducing vomiting right away (they will instruct you on the appropriate dosage for your dog).

DANGEROUS FOODS IN MY HOME

HIDDEN OR REMOVED

- [ ]
- [ ]
- [ ]
- [ ]
- [ ]
- [ ]
- [ ]
- [ ]
- [ ]
- [ ]
- [ ]
- [ ]
- [ ]

CHECKING
✻ VITAL SIGNS ✻

Vital signs are clinical measurements you can take that indicate the state of your puppy's essential body functions.

WHY WE CHECK VITAL SIGNS

Knowing how to check and record your puppy's "normal" vital signs gives you an important baseline of essential information if ever your puppy falls ill or has an accident. If you suspect that your puppy is sick and might need medical attention, you can take their vitals and compare them with the healthy stats you record here. The four main vitals to measure are: your puppy's heart rate, their breathing rate, their body temperature, and their hydration status/capillary refill time.

HOW TO MEASURE YOUR PUPPY'S VITALS

Heart Rate

STEP 1: With your puppy on his or her side, place one hand over their chest just behind the shoulder blade to feel their pulse. If you're having trouble, you can also try placing your fingers in the inner portion of your puppy's hind leg, right up against their body wall to feel a pulse through their femoral artery.

STEP 2: Count the number of heartbeats for 15 seconds and multiply that number by 4.

HELPFUL TIPS

- Remember to take your puppy's heart rate when they are resting and relaxed.
- A normal heart rate (in beats per minute) is between 60-140. Puppies, small dogs, and dogs that are out of shape will have faster heartbeats.
- It may be difficult at first to get the hang of taking your puppy's heart rate, so try it on a few different occasions to assess your puppy's baseline.
- Call your veterinarian if you have any concerns.

HEART RATE

DATE	RATE	DATE	RATE
DATE	RATE	DATE	RATE
DATE	RATE	DATE	RATE

Breathing Rate

STEP 1: Watch your puppy's chest or place a hand on their ribs while they are resting.

STEP 2: Count the number of times their chest expands in 15 seconds and multiply that number by 4.

HELPFUL TIPS

- A normal respiratory rate for a dog who isn't panting is between 10-35 breaths per minute.
- If your puppy is panting frantically and is glassy eyed, take them to emergency care right away.
- Normal breathing takes very little effort and produces little to no noise (unless you have a brachycephalic breed).
- Call your veterinarian if you have any concerns.

BREATHING RATE

DATE	RATE	DATE	RATE
DATE	RATE	DATE	RATE
DATE	RATE	DATE	RATE

Body Temperature

STEP 1: Lubricate the end of a rectal thermometer with a water-soluble lubricating jelly.

STEP 2: Have someone distract your puppy with treats and/or toys while you slowly insert the thermometer into your puppy's rectum, without force.

STEP 3: Once the thermometer stabilizes with a reading, remove it and record the results.

HELPFUL TIPS

- A normal temperature is between 100.5 - 102.5 degrees Fahrenheit.

- If you're not comfortable taking your puppy's temperature rectally, the next best option is to use an ear thermometer or a "touch-free" infrared thermometer specifically designed for animals.

- Call your veterinarian if you have any concerns.

BODY TEMPERATURE

DATE	TEMP	DATE	TEMP
DATE	TEMP	DATE	TEMP
DATE	TEMP	DATE	TEMP

Hydration Status/Capillary Refill Time

STEP 1: Gently pull back your puppy's upper lips and examine their gums, checking for a healthy pink color. With one finger, softly press on the gums and release. The depressed area should whiten and then return to the normal, pink color within roughly two seconds.

STEP 2: Gently pinch your puppy's skin behind and between their shoulder blades, lifting up as if to form a tent shape, then release. If the skin snaps back in under a second your puppy is adequately hydrated.

HELPFUL TIPS

- Dry, sticky or tacky-feeling gums may be a sign of dehydration.
- Some dog breeds have a black mouth pigmentation. If this is the case with your dog, focus on their tongue to assess hydration levels.
- Call your veterinarian if you have any concerns.

HYDRATION

DATE	GUM HEALTH	DATE	GUM HEALTH
DATE	GUM HEALTH	DATE	GUM HEALTH
DATE	GUM HEALTH	DATE	GUM HEALTH

PUPPY GROWTH TRACKER

AGE	WEIGHT	HEIGHT	LENGTH

NOTES

PUPPY TRAINING AND RAISING

FIRST MONTH AT A GLANCE

DAY 1

WELCOME HOME!
Topic:
Home Setup | Daily Routine

DAY 2

Topic: Housetraining | Crate Training
First Vet Appointment
Behavior Intro: Name Recognition
Mark the Moment

DAY 5

Topic:
Isolation Distress

DAY 6

Family & Friends Introduction

DAY 9

Behavior Intro:
Recall

DAY 10

Topic:
Puppy Communication

DAY 13

Topic:
Resource Guarding

DAY 14

DAY 17

New Game:
Catch Me if You Can

DAY 18

Behavior Intro:
Stay

DAY 21

New Game:
Fetch

DAY 22

Behavior Intro:
Sit

DAY 25

Behavior Intro:
Down

DAY 26

DAY 3 **Topic**: Socialization **Behavior Intro**: Go to your Crate	DAY 4 **New Game**: Follow the Leader **Topic**: Play-Biting | Barking & Whining
DAY 7 **New Game**: Seek **Topic**: Corrective Feedback	DAY 8 **Behavior Intro**: Lured Sit
DAY 11	DAY 12 **Behavior Intro**: Lured Down Leash Training
DAY 15 **Behavior Intro**: Touch	DAY 16 **Topic**: Jumping Up
DAY 19	DAY 20
DAY 23	DAY 24
DAY 27	DAY 28 **1 MONTH NEW PUPPY PARENT ANNIVERSARY!** Your Puppy has met or seen 50 new people

WEEK ONE: WELCOME HOME

INTRODUCTION

WHAT TO KNOW: PREPARING FOR THE WEEK AHEAD

The first week with your puppy can be an emotional rollercoaster. The pure joy and excitement of bringing your puppy home is tempered with midnight bathroom breaks, so it's completely normal to experience a wide range of emotions! Just remember that the first week will be one of the hardest as you and your puppy adjust to new routines and get to know each other. As you get up to speed on how to parent your new puppy, things will get easier. The number of sections in this program you need to read each week decreases as well to reflect that!

TO-DO LIST

	DONE
Develop your daily routine and set up your home	☐
SECTIONS TO READ	
First Vet Appointment	☐
Socialization	☐
Field Trips	☐
Housetraining	☐
Apartment Housetraining	☐
Crate Training	☐
Barking and Whining	☐
Play-Biting	☐
Isolation Distress	☐
Name Recognition	☐
Mark the Moment	☐
Corrective Feedback	☐
Games: "Follow the Leader" & "Seek"	☐

LEARNING OUTCOMES

The Focus of This Week Is On:

- 🐾 Bonding with your puppy.
- 🐾 Setting up your home to ease into the transition of puppy parenthood and make your puppy more comfortable in their new environment.
- 🐾 Establishing your daily routine.
- 🐾 Laying the foundation for your puppy to effectively learn basic obedience by teaching them a "Mark the Moment" word.

BY THE END OF THIS WEEK YOUR PUPPY SHOULD:

- ⊘ *Understand where their bathroom area is by consistently using it when you place them there for a bathroom break.*

- ⊘ *Be comfortable going in and out of their crate and eating there.*

- ⊘ *Recognize the value of their name by turning towards you in anticipation when you call it.*

- ⊘ *Respond enthusiastically to "Yes", the "Mark the Moment" word in anticipation of a reward.*

- ⊘ *Have interacted with or seen 15-20 family members and friends.*

WEEK 1 CURRICULUM
❖ WELCOME HOME ❖

10-MINUTE MORNING TRAINING SESSIONS

DAY 1	☐ Welcome home! Enjoy showing your puppy their new home and introducing them to their family
DAY 2	☐ Practice "Name Recognition": 10 repetitions ☐ Practice dropping treats inside and outside of your puppy's crate to encourage them to go in and out of it
DAY 3	☐ Practice "Name Recognition": 10 repetitions ☐ Practice "Go to your Crate": 10 repetitions
DAY 4	☐ Practice "Go to your Crate": 10 repetitions
DAY 5	☐ Practice "Go to your Crate": 10 repetitions
DAY 6	☐ Practice "Mark the Moment": 20 repetitions ☐ Practice "Name Recognition": 10 repetitions
DAY 7	☐ Practice "Mark the Moment": 20 repetitions

GAMES TO INCORPORATE INTO PLAYTIME THIS WEEK

"Follow the Leader" | "Seek"

10-MINUTE AFTERNOON TRAINING SESSIONS

DAY 1	☐ Introduce your puppy to their crate by dropping treats inside and around it ☐ Place a stuffed chew toy or bone inside or outside of your puppy's crate for them to enjoy
DAY 2	☐ Practice "Mark the Moment": 20 repetitions ☐ Practice "Name Recognition": 10 repetitions ☐ Practice dropping treats inside and outside of your puppy's crate to encourage them to go in and out of it
DAY 3	☐ Practice "Mark the Moment": 20 repetitions ☐ Practice "Name Recognition": 10 repetitions ☐ Practice "Go to your Crate": 10 repetitions
DAY 4	☐ Practice "Mark the Moment": 20 repetitions ☐ Practice "Name Recognition": 10 repetitions ☐ Practice "Go to your Crate": 10 repetitions
DAY 5	☐ Practice "Mark the Moment": 20 repetitions ☐ Practice "Name Recognition": 10 repetitions ☐ Practice "Go to your Crate": 10 repetitions
DAY 6	☐ Practice "Mark the Moment": 20 repetitions ☐ Practice "Name Recognition": 10 repetitions ☐ Practice "Go to your Crate": 10 repetitions
DAY 7	☐ Practice "Mark the Moment": 20 repetitions ☐ Practice "Go to your Crate": 10 repetitions

FIELD TRIPS

- [ ] Take your puppy on 2 car rides.

SOCIALIZATION

- [ ] Perform a handling routine.
- [ ] Cradle your puppy in your arms on their back (like you would hold a newborn baby).
- [ ] Put your puppy's collar and harness on.
- [ ] Grab your puppy's collar and release it.
- [ ] Let your puppy sniff their brush and grooming equipment.
- [ ] Introduce your puppy to any other household pets.
- [ ] Use common household appliances around your puppy.
- [ ] Place or walk your puppy on slippery and hard surfaces.
- [ ] Expose your puppy to everyday household objects.
- [ ] Introduce your puppy to close friends and members of your extended family at the end of the first week.

HELPFUL TIPS

- 🐾 Don't overwhelm your puppy on their first day home by having visitors over; wait until later in the week.
- 🐾 Letting your puppy out of the crate when they whine reinforces their whining and teaches them to repeat that behavior when they want to get out of their crate.
- 🐾 If you catch your puppy having an accident inside the house, interrupt them in the act and take them to their bathroom area.
- 🐾 Whining, circling, sniffing, and barking are all signs your puppy needs to go to the bathroom.

DEVELOPING GOOD DAILY HABITS

	M	T	W	T	F	S	S
Follow your puppy's daily routine.	☐	☐	☐	☐	☐	☐	☐
Use your housetraining verbal cue word and take your puppy to the exact same area every time they need to relieve themselves.	☐	☐	☐	☐	☐	☐	☐
Feed your puppy 4 hours before you go to bed and take away their water 1-2 hours before you go to bed.	☐	☐	☐	☐	☐	☐	☐
Take away your puppy's food between meals and pick up bowls 10 minutes after you have placed them down; make a note of how much food, if any is left over.	☐	☐	☐	☐	☐	☐	☐
Feed your puppy the majority of their meals in their crate with the door open.	☐	☐	☐	☐	☐	☐	☐
Place your puppy in their crate, exercise pen, puppy room, or have them tethered to you with a leash anytime you can't actively supervise them.	☐	☐	☐	☐	☐	☐	☐
Place your puppy in their crate when they are tired or ready to sleep.	☐	☐	☐	☐	☐	☐	☐
Don't let your puppy out of their crate if they are whining or barking; wait for a quiet moment.	☐	☐	☐	☐	☐	☐	☐
Put your puppy in their crate, exercise pen, or puppy room for some alone time and refer to the isolation distress section for creating positive alone experiences.	☐	☐	☐	☐	☐	☐	☐

FIRST VETERINARIAN ❧ APPOINTMENT ❧

WHAT TO BRING

- Any medical/vaccination records you have for your puppy.
- Stool sample (confirm when booking your appointment that this is needed).
- Brand name of your puppy's food.

WHAT TO EXPECT

A THOROUGH PHYSICAL EXAM WHERE YOUR VET WILL:

- Listen to your puppy's heart and lungs.
- Check your puppy's ears, eyes, skin, coat, anal glands, hydration status, nails, muscles and fat deposits.
- Palpate your puppy's knees, hips, and lymph nodes.
- Examine the alignment of your puppy's teeth.
- Feel your puppy's abdomen.
- Perform a rectal exam.
- Weigh your puppy.

PUPPY TRAINING AND RAISING

VACCINATIONS: Guidance on what vaccinations your puppy needs and your vet will administer any that are immediately required.

DEWORMING: A fecal exam may be done to determine if your puppy needs deworming medication.

MICROCHIPPING: Your vet will recommend that your puppy receive an electronic ID tag so they can be easily identified and returned to you, if lost.

DISCUSSION: Your vet will discuss your puppy's history and any questions you may have about feeding, nutrition, medical issues, vaccinations, training, socialization and future care requirements.

QUESTIONS TO ASK

1. What food do you recommend for my puppy and should I be considering supplements?
2. What non-core vaccinations should I be considering for my puppy?
3. Do you have any breed-specific medical advice? What things should I look out for and/or be aware of?
4. What are the risks of bringing a puppy who hasn't completed their vaccinations to a public place versus the risks of under-socialization? In your opinion, which risk is a greater threat to my puppy?
5. (If you plan on traveling or moving with your puppy) Are there specific vaccination requirements and documents my puppy will need to go to (insert name of a country)?

HELPFUL TIPS

- Schedule your puppy's vet appointment early in the day. If your puppy has an allergic reaction to the vaccinations, it's less likely you'll have to take them to the emergency room in the middle of the night.

VACCINATION SCHEDULE EXAMPLE

AGE	RECOMMENDED VACCINES	OPTIONAL VACCINES
6-8 WEEKS	DHPP (Distemper | Infectious hepatitis | Parainfluenza | Parvovirus)	Bordetella | Measles
8-12 WEEKS	DHPP	Coronavirus | Leptospirosis, Bordetella | Lyme Disease
12-24 WEEKS	Rabies	None
14-16 WEEKS	DHPP	Coronavirus | Lyme disease Leptospirosis
12-16 MONTHS	Rabies | DHPP	Coronavirus | Leptospirosis Bordetella | Lyme Disease
ANNUAL	None	Coronavirus | Leptospirosis Bordetella | Lyme Disease
1ST YEAR BOOSTER	DHHP	None
EVERY 3 YEARS	DHHP	None
EVERY 1-3 YEARS	Rabies (as required by law)	None

PUPPY TRAINING AND RAISING

FIRST APPOINTMENT DATE

VETERINARIAN RECOMMENDATIONS

SOCIALIZATION

Socialization is the process of conditioning your puppy to enjoy interactions and be comfortable with other people, animals, objects, places and everyday activities.

WHY WE SOCIALIZE PUPPIES

A lack of early socialization in puppies is a leading cause of behavioral issues that develop in adolescence and adulthood. Common problems include:

LEERY OF NEW PEOPLE: Any encounter with an unfamiliar face results in a range of unwanted behaviors like retreating, cowering, barking, growling, or even lunging toward the stranger.

DOG AGGRESSION: Friendly approaches and interactions from other dogs are met with aggressive responses.

REACTIVITY: Everyday stimuli, whether it be a person, a dog, a cyclist, or trash can trigger an aggressive and unwarranted response.

CRIPPLING ANXIETY: Exposure to anything unfamiliar results in an unwillingness to engage.

DIFFICULTY HANDLING: Basic grooming like nail trimming and brushing teeth become impossible to accomplish without professional assistance.

FEAR OF THE OUTDOORS: Leaving the security of home becomes a frightening and unpredictable gamble that dogs hope to avoid.

SOUND SENSITIVITY: Common sounds, from vacuum cleaners to toilets flushing, become distressing alarms that can go off at any moment.

HOW TO SOCIALIZE YOUR PUPPY

STEP 1 — *Over the course of each week, go through each experience on the socialization checklist and, with treats in hand, carefully introduce your puppy to those experiences.*

STEP 2 — *Repeatedly hand feed your puppy treats during each of the socialization experiences to help your puppy build confidence and create positive associations.*

GOAL AFTER EACH EXPERIENCE

Your objective with each experience is to give your puppy the confidence and comfort to feel good about aspects of daily life that your puppy will encounter inside and outside of the house.

NOTES

SOCIALIZATION RULES

1. To start, keep each socialization experience to 15 minutes or less.
2. Never force a physical interaction on your puppy if they are nervous or fearful. Always create space for them to withdraw from a situation they find uncomfortable.
3. Do not coddle, pet, or reassure your puppy if they are acting nervous and fearful as this will only reinforce this fearful behavior and not help them build confidence.
4. Your puppy can be effectively socialized to other people, animals and objects without having to directly interact with them. This is especially useful when it comes to naturally timid and shy puppies.
5. Socialization will only have a positive effect if the experience itself is positive; watch your puppy's body language for signs of distress and provide treats throughout the experience.

HANDLING ROUTINE

One of the activities in the weekly socialization checklist is to perform a handling routine. Here's how to do it:

Sit down with your puppy and hold or handle the following body parts for a second or two.

- One ear » treat; Other ear » treat
- Paw squeeze » treat; Paw squeeze » treat; Paw squeeze » treat; Paw squeeze » treat
- Open mouth » treat
- Run your hand down the length of their body and tail » treat
- Look in their eyes » treat
- Hug » treat

TROUBLESHOOTING

- If your puppy is nervous or fearful during a socialization activity, stop and try again another time. Depending on the situation, you may want to let your puppy observe from a greater distance, gradually moving closer over time as your puppy gains confidence. It is important that you take the time to work through your puppy's apprehension - most puppies don't just "grow out of it", they need to work through it with your help.

- If your puppy pulls away while you're doing your handling exercises, gently hold them in place. Say "Nope" in a gentle, neutral way and wait for them to stop pulling. When they relax, say "Yes" and hand them a treat.

HELPFUL TIPS

- Take your puppy for a bathroom break before going to a public place and consider giving treats to friendly strangers to give to your puppy.

- The treats you feed your puppy during socialization play an important role in conditioning a positive emotional response to any new experience.

- Socializing your puppy with just two or three puppies and/or dogs is not enough. They need exposure to as many puppies and/or dogs as possible.

SOCIALIZATION PROGRESS

PEOPLE

WEEK	PROGRESS
1	1 | 2 | 3 | 4 | 5
2	1 | 2 | 3 | 4 | 5
3	1 | 2 | 3 | 4 | 5
4	1 | 2 | 3 | 4 | 5
5	1 | 2 | 3 | 4 | 5
6	1 | 2 | 3 | 4 | 5
7	1 | 2 | 3 | 4 | 5
8	1 | 2 | 3 | 4 | 5

DOGS | PUPPIES

WEEK	PROGRESS
1	1 | 2 | 3 | 4 | 5
2	1 | 2 | 3 | 4 | 5
3	1 | 2 | 3 | 4 | 5
4	1 | 2 | 3 | 4 | 5
5	1 | 2 | 3 | 4 | 5
6	1 | 2 | 3 | 4 | 5
7	1 | 2 | 3 | 4 | 5
8	1 | 2 | 3 | 4 | 5

(1 = Still Getting Comfortable, 5 = Comfortable)

OTHER ANIMALS

WEEK	PROGRESS
1	1 | 2 | 3 | 4 | 5
2	1 | 2 | 3 | 4 | 5
3	1 | 2 | 3 | 4 | 5
4	1 | 2 | 3 | 4 | 5
5	1 | 2 | 3 | 4 | 5
6	1 | 2 | 3 | 4 | 5
7	1 | 2 | 3 | 4 | 5
8	1 | 2 | 3 | 4 | 5

SOUNDS

WEEK	PROGRESS
1	1 | 2 | 3 | 4 | 5
2	1 | 2 | 3 | 4 | 5
3	1 | 2 | 3 | 4 | 5
4	1 | 2 | 3 | 4 | 5
5	1 | 2 | 3 | 4 | 5
6	1 | 2 | 3 | 4 | 5
7	1 | 2 | 3 | 4 | 5
8	1 | 2 | 3 | 4 | 5

(1 = Still Getting Comfortable, 5 = Comfortable)

SURFACES

WEEK	PROGRESS
1	1 | 2 | 3 | 4 | 5
2	1 | 2 | 3 | 4 | 5
3	1 | 2 | 3 | 4 | 5
4	1 | 2 | 3 | 4 | 5
5	1 | 2 | 3 | 4 | 5
6	1 | 2 | 3 | 4 | 5
7	1 | 2 | 3 | 4 | 5
8	1 | 2 | 3 | 4 | 5

VEHICLES

WEEK	PROGRESS
1	1 | 2 | 3 | 4 | 5
2	1 | 2 | 3 | 4 | 5
3	1 | 2 | 3 | 4 | 5
4	1 | 2 | 3 | 4 | 5
5	1 | 2 | 3 | 4 | 5
6	1 | 2 | 3 | 4 | 5
7	1 | 2 | 3 | 4 | 5
8	1 | 2 | 3 | 4 | 5

(1 = Still Getting Comfortable, 5 = Comfortable)

MOVING OBJECTS & PEOPLE

WEEK	PROGRESS
1	1 | 2 | 3 | 4 | 5
2	1 | 2 | 3 | 4 | 5
3	1 | 2 | 3 | 4 | 5
4	1 | 2 | 3 | 4 | 5
5	1 | 2 | 3 | 4 | 5
6	1 | 2 | 3 | 4 | 5
7	1 | 2 | 3 | 4 | 5
8	1 | 2 | 3 | 4 | 5

EVERYDAY OBJECTS

WEEK	PROGRESS
1	1 | 2 | 3 | 4 | 5
2	1 | 2 | 3 | 4 | 5
3	1 | 2 | 3 | 4 | 5
4	1 | 2 | 3 | 4 | 5
5	1 | 2 | 3 | 4 | 5
6	1 | 2 | 3 | 4 | 5
7	1 | 2 | 3 | 4 | 5
8	1 | 2 | 3 | 4 | 5

(1 = Still Getting Comfortable, 5 = Comfortable)

FIELD TRIPS

Field trips are short outings with your puppy in a safe and controlled manner, minimizing the risk of contracting an infectious disease while exposing your puppy to common elements of their broader environment.

WHY GO ON FIELD TRIPS?

Field trips are a good way to thoroughly socialize your puppy during the sensitive socialization period so they grow up to be a confident and well-adjusted adult dog.

FIELD TRIP RULES

For puppies that haven't completed their vaccination series and are still at risk for contracting infectious diseases:

1. Carry your puppy to and from your destination.
2. Keep your puppy on your lap or in a travel carrier. Don't put them on the ground.
3. Prohibit any interaction with strange dogs.
4. Make sure all dogs your puppy interacts with are up-to-date on their vaccinations.
5. Completely avoid visits to dog parks or other areas that are not sanitized and/or are highly trafficked by dogs.

FIELD TRIP LOG
HOW DID YOUR PUPPY ENJOY THEIR TRIP?

TRIP	NOTES
CAR RIDE	Drive-thru
COFFEE SHOP *Restaurant*	
PUPPY CLASS	
NIGHT TIME CAR RIDE	
SHOPPING CENTER	
FRIEND'S HOUSE	
NIGHT WALK	
EVENT *Breweries*	
FOREST WALK *Beach*	

HOUSETRAINING

WHY WE HOUSETRAIN PUPPIES

Your puppy will not instinctively understand where they are supposed to relieve themselves. They need you to teach them where they should and should not go.

HOW TO HOUSETRAIN YOUR PUPPY

STEP 1	*Start by getting your puppy comfortable in their crate (read the crate training section for guidance). Ensure that your puppy is sleeping and taking every nap in their crate. If they fall asleep outside of their crate, scoop them up and place them inside the crate.*
STEP 2	*Consistently follow your daily routine, giving your puppy regular opportunities to relieve themselves. Until they no longer have any accidents, do not let your puppy wander around freely in your home. If you can't actively watch them, place them in their crate.*
STEP 3	*Bring your puppy to their bathroom area when they wake up in the morning, after any nap, after play and/or training sessions, 15-20 minutes after eating or drinking, and anytime you take them out of their crate.*
STEP 4	*When you bring your puppy outside to relieve themselves, say "Outside" as you open the door and then place them in their specific bathroom area and say "Go Potty". Stand next to them until they go.*
STEP 5	*When your puppy starts to relieve themselves, say "Yes" and then give them treats along with enthusiastic praise when they are finished.*

> 🏆 **VERBAL CUE WORD: "GO POTTY"**

TROUBLESHOOTING

🦴 If your puppy keeps having accidents, give them more opportunities throughout the day to relieve themselves and, between potty breaks, make sure they are confined when unsupervised. The most common cause of bathroom-related accidents is a lack of supervision coupled with too much freedom in the house.

🦴 If the accidents are always in the same place, make sure to use a good enzyme cleaner to clear up accidents. Puppies will naturally gravitate to any scent of urine as a cue that this is where the bathroom is.

🦴 If your puppy keeps having accidents inside their crate:

1. *Check with your vet to rule out medical issues related to bladder and bowel control.*
2. *Ensure that your crate is only big enough for your puppy to get up and turn around in (any bigger and they will use one end as a toilet).*
3. *Reduce the amount of time your puppy spends crated before having the opportunity to get out and relieve themselves.*

🦴 If you catch your puppy having an accident, try stopping them in the act by saying "No" and clapping loudly to startle them, then immediately take them to their bathroom area. Never punish your puppy for accidents that happened in the past; they will not understand why you are punishing them.

🦴 If your puppy tries to engage you in play when taking them to their bathroom area, ignore them. If they try to explore, put them on a leash to prevent them from leaving their potty area. If your puppy still hasn't relieved themselves after 10 minutes, put them back in their crate for 5-10 minutes and then try again.

- If your puppy refuses to go to the bathroom in their designated area, look for another area that is quieter or more private, provides some protection from the elements (toy breeds often refuse to relieve themselves in cold and wet environments), and is their preferred surface (grass, concrete, gravel, etc).

- If your puppy wants to play after a midnight bathroom break, try turning on fewer lights in the house and ignore the attempts to engage you.

HELPFUL TIPS

- The general rule of thumb is that puppies can "hold it" for one hour per month of age plus one: at one month your puppy can wait 1-2 hours, at two months your puppy can wait 2-3 hours, and so on.

- Until four months of age, puppies generally need ten or more opportunities to relieve themselves over the course of the day. The more frequently you take them to their bathroom area, the more quickly they will learn to relieve themselves in that area.

- Circling and sniffing the ground is an indication your puppy may need to relieve themselves.

HOUSETRAINING PROGRESS

WEEK	NOTES / # ACCIDENTS
1	
2	
3	
4	
5	
6	
7	
8	

APARTMENT HOUSETRAINING

STEP 1	Start by getting your puppy comfortable in their crate (read the crate training section for guidance). Ensure that your puppy is sleeping and taking every nap in their crate. If they fall asleep outside of their crate, scoop them up and place them inside the crate.
STEP 2	Consistently follow your daily routine, giving your puppy regular opportunities to relieve themselves. Until they no longer have any accidents, do not let your puppy wander around freely in your home. If you can't actively watch them, place them in their crate.
STEP 3	Bring your puppy to their bathroom area when they wake up in the morning, after any nap, after play and/or training sessions, 15-20 minutes after eating or drinking, and anytime you take them out of their crate.
STEP 4	When you bring your puppy to their bathroom area, use your housetraining cue word, and stay next to them until they go.
STEP 5	When your puppy starts to relieve themselves, say "Yes" and then give them treats along with enthusiastic praise when they are finished.
STEP 6	When you start transitioning your puppy's housetraining outside, bring a used pee pad or training turf with you and place your puppy down on it outside following the same instructions as above.
STEP 7	Begin phasing out the use of a pee pad or training turf when your puppy starts to get the hang of relieving themselves outside.

> 🏆 **VERBAL CUE WORD: "GO POTTY"**

TROUBLESHOOTING

Read through the troubleshooting tips on the Housetraining (page 75).

HELPFUL TIPS

- It's common for puppies that live in apartments to start housetraining inside because they don't have the bladder and/or bowel control to make it out of the building without having an accident. In addition, until your puppy is fully vaccinated, it may not be safe to take them to an area where other residents and neighbors take their dogs for bathroom breaks.

- The decision to initially train your puppy using a pee pad or training turf should, in part, be based on what surface your puppy will likely be relieving themselves on when you start training them outside. For example, if you live in a downtown high-rise and they will be relieving themselves on a concrete surface outdoors, then a pee pad is prefered over training turf.

❈ BATHROOM HISTORY ❈

Keeping track of your puppy's bathroom habits can be very useful if your puppy is struggling with housetraining. It will allow you to see patterns and adjust your daily routine to give them more opportunities to relieve themselves in desired places.

DAY 1	Time ___ Poop ☐ Pee ☐ Accident Y | N	Time ___ Poop ☐ Pee ☐ Accident Y | N	Time ___ Poop ☐ Pee ☐ Accident Y | N	Time ___ Poop ☐ Pee ☐ Accident Y | N	Time ___ Poop ☐ Pee ☐ Accident Y | N
DAY 2	Time ___ Poop ☐ Pee ☐ Accident Y | N	Time ___ Poop ☐ Pee ☐ Accident Y | N	Time ___ Poop ☐ Pee ☐ Accident Y | N	Time ___ Poop ☐ Pee ☐ Accident Y | N	Time ___ Poop ☐ Pee ☐ Accident Y | N
DAY 3	Time ___ Poop ☐ Pee ☐ Accident Y | N	Time ___ Poop ☐ Pee ☐ Accident Y | N	Time ___ Poop ☐ Pee ☐ Accident Y | N	Time ___ Poop ☐ Pee ☐ Accident Y | N	Time ___ Poop ☐ Pee ☐ Accident Y | N
DAY 4	Time ___ Poop ☐ Pee ☐ Accident Y | N	Time ___ Poop ☐ Pee ☐ Accident Y | N	Time ___ Poop ☐ Pee ☐ Accident Y | N	Time ___ Poop ☐ Pee ☐ Accident Y | N	Time ___ Poop ☐ Pee ☐ Accident Y | N
DAY 5	Time ___ Poop ☐ Pee ☐ Accident Y | N	Time ___ Poop ☐ Pee ☐ Accident Y | N	Time ___ Poop ☐ Pee ☐ Accident Y | N	Time ___ Poop ☐ Pee ☐ Accident Y | N	Time ___ Poop ☐ Pee ☐ Accident Y | N
DAY 6	Time ___ Poop ☐ Pee ☐ Accident Y | N	Time ___ Poop ☐ Pee ☐ Accident Y | N	Time ___ Poop ☐ Pee ☐ Accident Y | N	Time ___ Poop ☐ Pee ☐ Accident Y | N	Time ___ Poop ☐ Pee ☐ Accident Y | N
DAY 7	Time ___ Poop ☐ Pee ☐ Accident Y | N	Time ___ Poop ☐ Pee ☐ Accident Y | N	Time ___ Poop ☐ Pee ☐ Accident Y | N	Time ___ Poop ☐ Pee ☐ Accident Y | N	Time ___ Poop ☐ Pee ☐ Accident Y | N

Time ____ Poop ☐ Pee ☐ Accident Y | N	Time ____ Poop ☐ Pee ☐ Accident Y | N	Time ____ Poop ☐ Pee ☐ Accident Y | N	Time ____ Poop ☐ Pee ☐ Accident Y | N	Time ____ Poop ☐ Pee ☐ Accident Y | N
Time ____ Poop ☐ Pee ☐ Accident Y | N	Time ____ Poop ☐ Pee ☐ Accident Y | N	Time ____ Poop ☐ Pee ☐ Accident Y | N	Time ____ Poop ☐ Pee ☐ Accident Y | N	Time ____ Poop ☐ Pee ☐ Accident Y | N
Time ____ Poop ☐ Pee ☐ Accident Y | N	Time ____ Poop ☐ Pee ☐ Accident Y | N	Time ____ Poop ☐ Pee ☐ Accident Y | N	Time ____ Poop ☐ Pee ☐ Accident Y | N	Time ____ Poop ☐ Pee ☐ Accident Y | N
Time ____ Poop ☐ Pee ☐ Accident Y | N	Time ____ Poop ☐ Pee ☐ Accident Y | N	Time ____ Poop ☐ Pee ☐ Accident Y | N	Time ____ Poop ☐ Pee ☐ Accident Y | N	Time ____ Poop ☐ Pee ☐ Accident Y | N
Time ____ Poop ☐ Pee ☐ Accident Y | N	Time ____ Poop ☐ Pee ☐ Accident Y | N	Time ____ Poop ☐ Pee ☐ Accident Y | N	Time ____ Poop ☐ Pee ☐ Accident Y | N	Time ____ Poop ☐ Pee ☐ Accident Y | N
Time ____ Poop ☐ Pee ☐ Accident Y | N	Time ____ Poop ☐ Pee ☐ Accident Y | N	Time ____ Poop ☐ Pee ☐ Accident Y | N	Time ____ Poop ☐ Pee ☐ Accident Y | N	Time ____ Poop ☐ Pee ☐ Accident Y | N
Time ____ Poop ☐ Pee ☐ Accident Y | N	Time ____ Poop ☐ Pee ☐ Accident Y | N	Time ____ Poop ☐ Pee ☐ Accident Y | N	Time ____ Poop ☐ Pee ☐ Accident Y | N	Time ____ Poop ☐ Pee ☐ Accident Y | N

CRATE TRAINING

Crate training is the process of habituating your puppy to their crate by creating positive associations and a sense of security, safety, and comfort.

WHY WE CRATE TRAIN PUPPIES

There are many benefits to crate training your puppy but chief among them is that it greatly increases the likelihood of successful housetraining. Puppies will naturally avoid relieving themselves in their bed, if possible, and actively try to "hold it" until you let them out of their crate. Crates also give puppies a safe space to retreat to when they want to relax and have some quiet time. Finally, a crate trained dog is easier to travel with, making trips to the groomer, vet, or daycare a breeze.

IS A CRATE PUPPY JAIL?

Absolutely not! Dogs are denning animals; they like small, close and dark spaces. That's why you will often find dogs resting under tables and chairs, burrowing under blankets, and stretching out behind a couch. Humans like wide open, light and bright spaces. Dogs don't. Your puppy will not consider their crate a jail. If introduced in the right way and not used as a place of punishment, it will be one of their favorite places to hang out.

ACTIVITIES TO GET YOUR PUPPY COMFORTABLE WITH THEIR CRATE

- During the day, put the crate in an area of the house that isn't isolated from the rest of the family; leave the gate open and let your puppy explore it while you are watching them.

- Invite your puppy over to the crate and drop treats just outside the gate and at the back of the crate. Continue to drop treats inside the crate until your puppy will calmly enter and exit.

- Feed your puppy all their meals inside the crate (with the exception of a few meals used in training sessions specified in your weekly training program). For the first week, leave the door of the crate open while they eat. After the first week, close the door while your puppy eats but open it up as soon as they finish. Gradually increase the length of time you leave the door closed after they finish eating.

- Once a day, place your puppy in their crate and give them a chew toy stuffed with treats or a bully stick to play with. Start by leaving the door open but, as your puppy becomes more comfortable with their crate, you can eventually close it.

- If your puppy falls asleep outside of the crate, scoop them up and place them in their crate (and close the door).

HOW TO TEACH YOUR PUPPY
"GO TO YOUR CRATE"

STEP 1 — Say "Crate" and toss a treat into the crate, followed by "Yes" as soon as your puppy steps into the crate to retrieve the treat. Repeat until your puppy enthusiastically and reliably goes into their crate to retrieve the treat. This may take a few training sessions.

STEP 2 — Distract your puppy with a treat and, when they aren't looking, toss a treat into the crate. Say "Crate" and gesture as if you were going to toss a treat into the crate (but don't actually toss the treat). After your puppy goes in and is done eating the treat you previously threw, you can feed them a few more treats while they are inside the crate and say "Yes".

STEP 3 — Repeat step 2 but, instead of leaving the door open when your puppy goes inside the crate, close the door behind them and feed them treats through the gate. Make them wait a few moments before opening the door again and saying "Yes".

STEP 4 — Build on the length of time you leave your puppy with a closed door until they can handle being there for longer periods. Outside of nap times, it's also okay to randomly drop treats into the crate while the door is closed.

STEP 5 — Introduce the "Wait" command to prevent your puppy from rushing out of the crate whenever the door is opened. Slowly open the crate door and say "Wait". If your puppy starts to push their way out as the door opens, close it back. Repeat the cue word "Wait" and try opening the door again, closing the door if your puppy starts to push their way out. Once your puppy is nicely waiting, open the door fully and say "Yes" and reward them with a treat.

VERBAL CUE WORD: "CRATE"

CRATE RULES

1. Don't force your crate on your puppy, give them time to go willingingly. For some puppies this will take a few minutes, for others a few days. Patience is key.

2. Avoid using the crate as a form of punishment; your puppy will come to fear it and refuse to use it.

3. For safety reasons, make sure your puppy has nothing on when you leave them in their crate unattended.

4. Don't leave food in the crate. Your puppy should be on routine timed feedings and should never be in the crate so long that they require food. The only exception to this is a chew toy stuffed with treats, used as a training tool to help create positive associations with the crate. If you're away for a longer period, use a puppy room or exercise pen that houses their crate (with the door open), food, water, a safe chew toy, and a bathroom area.

5. Exceptional circumstances aside, you should rarely need to provide your puppy with water if they are being crated for less than 2 hours. If you need to crate them for much longer, consider using a doggie water bottle intended for crate use.

6. Always give your puppy a bathroom break before putting them in their crate.

TROUBLESHOOTING

- It's normal for puppies to whine at nap or bedtime for a few minutes or so, as long as they've gone to the bathroom, enjoyed some mental and physical exercise, and had food and water, they will eventually settle and go to sleep.

- Outside of naptime, to stop your puppy from whining and barking of boredom in their crate, give them a stuffed chew toy, bone, or a puzzle toy.

- Always wait for a quiet moment before letting your puppy out of the crate to avoid reinforcing the negative behavior.

- If your puppy is struggling to settle in a wire crate because they are over-stimulated by their surroundings, drape a blanket over the crate (leaving a portion uncovered for sufficient airflow). Alternatively, you might also consider switching to a plastic crate.

- If your puppy lacks enthusiasm when you are teaching them to "Go to Your Crate", you can lightly restrain them for a few seconds while they watch you toss a treat into the crate. Preventing them from initially retrieving the treat builds their drive and enthusiasm to go into the crate to get it.

HELPFUL TIPS

- A puppy who is 3-6 months of age can typically be crated for 3 to 4 hours at a time during the day once they are comfortable with the crate, assuming they've been fed, exercised, and taken to the bathroom first.

- Consider tying the crate door open when you're first introducing the crate to your puppy so they don't accidentally get hit by the door when they enter the crate and get scared.

- For the first year it's a good idea to occasionally crate your puppy for short periods while you are home so they don't associate crating with being left alone.

"GO TO YOUR CRATE" PROGRESS

WEEK	PROGRESS
1	1 | 2 | 3 | 4 | 5
2	1 | 2 | 3 | 4 | 5
3	1 | 2 | 3 | 4 | 5
4	1 | 2 | 3 | 4 | 5
5	1 | 2 | 3 | 4 | 5
6	1 | 2 | 3 | 4 | 5
7	1 | 2 | 3 | 4 | 5
8	1 | 2 | 3 | 4 | 5

(1 = Learning, 5 = Perfected)

PUPPY'S CRATE COMFORT LEVEL

WEEK	PUPPY'S CRATE COMFORT LEVEL
1	1 | 2 | 3 | 4 | 5
2	1 | 2 | 3 | 4 | 5
3	1 | 2 | 3 | 4 | 5
4	1 | 2 | 3 | 4 | 5
5	1 | 2 | 3 | 4 | 5
6	1 | 2 | 3 | 4 | 5
7	1 | 2 | 3 | 4 | 5
8	1 | 2 | 3 | 4 | 5

(1 = Not Comfortable, 5 = Comfortable)

BARKING & WHINING

WHY WE TEACH PUPPIES WHEN THEY SHOULD AND SHOULDN'T BARK

There are times when you may want your puppy to bark - telling you when they need to go to the bathroom or alerting you to strangers. Often though, barking and whining is a nuisance behavior that gets quickly reinforced by puppy parents.

HOW TO KEEP YOUR PUPPY FROM BARKING AND WHINING IN THE CRATE WHEN YOU'RE NEARBY

STEP 1	*Do the exercises provided in the crate training section to condition your puppy to love spending time in their crate.*
STEP 2	*Before placing your puppy in their crate, make sure they've gone to the bathroom and had some exercise. Place a toy, bone, or stuffed chew toy in the crate to give them something to do if it's not naptime.*
STEP 3	*Once your puppy is inside the crate, do not engage them. Avoid talking or looking at them.*
STEP 4	*Ignore all whining and barking, letting your puppy "bark it out".*
STEP 5	*Once your puppy is quiet, drop treats in the crate at random intervals to reward them for their quiet behavior.*

TROUBLESHOOTING

🦴 If your puppy's whining and barking persists, cover the crate with a light blanket so they can't see out (leaving enough of an opening for airflow) and play some relaxing music or white noise.

🦴 If your puppy barks and whines in their crate only when you leave the room, this is a signal they may be experiencing isolation distress (see the isolation distress section to address this behavior).

🦴 If your puppy continues to bark and whine, say "Quiet" and tap gently on the side of their crate. Repeat as necessary. Reward quiet behavior by dropping treats in their crate.

HELPFUL TIPS

🐾 Good earplugs or noise cancelling headphones can help you resist the urge to let your puppy out of the crate when they are whining and barking.

🐾 Try to wait 3-5 minutes after your puppy has quieted down before letting them out to avoid rewarding their noisy behavior.

PUPPY'S NOISE LEVEL IN THE CRATE

WEEK	PROGRESS
1	1 | 2 | 3 | 4 | 5
2	1 | 2 | 3 | 4 | 5
3	1 | 2 | 3 | 4 | 5
4	1 | 2 | 3 | 4 | 5
5	1 | 2 | 3 | 4 | 5
6	1 | 2 | 3 | 4 | 5
7	1 | 2 | 3 | 4 | 5
8	1 | 2 | 3 | 4 | 5

(1 = Loud, 5 = Quiet)

HOW TO STOP YOUR PUPPY FROM BARKING AND WHINING WHEN YOU LEAVE

STEP 1 — Do the exercises provided in the crate training section to condition your puppy to love spending time in their crate.

STEP 2 — Practice giving your puppy plenty of time alone in their crate, exercise pen, or puppy room while you are at home but out of sight.

STEP 3 — Make sure your puppy has had enough mental and physical exercise, and a bathroom break, before you leave.

STEP 4 — Put your puppy in their crate, exercise pen, or puppy room with a chew toy stuffed with treats at least five minutes before leaving the house.

STEP 5 — Don't prolong your departure or make it an emotional goodbye and, when you return home, avoid rewarding your puppy for their excitement with too much enthusiasm.

STEP 6 — The first few times you leave, try keeping your outings under an hour.

TROUBLESHOOTING

- Consider playing some soothing music to block out outdoor noise when you leave the house.

- Freezing a Kong toy stuffed with softened kibble and peanut butter will give your puppy a tasty distraction while you are out.

HELPFUL TIPS

- 🐾 Keeping departures and arrivals calm reduces the overall anxiety for your puppy and allows them to relax instead of anxiously awaiting your return.

- 🐾 Offering your puppy a high value reward (like a chew toy stuffed with treats) before you leave helps them associate your absence with positive emotions.

NOTES

PLAY-BITING

Play-biting is a natural puppy behavior where they will nip and bite people and/or dogs as a form of social play. It's one of their favorite things to do and is totally normal.

WHY WE TEACH PUPPIES BITE INHIBITION

Play-biting can be uncomfortable or even painful, depending on the circumstances, so it's important for dogs to learn how to control their bite. Developmentally, puppyhood is the only time this can be done, so it's important to give your puppy plenty of feedback about their bite intensity and strength early and often. Teaching them to inhibit their bite will ensure that they have a soft and safe mouth as an adult, and it's an essential part of raising a trustworthy well-behaved puppy.

HOW TO TEACH YOUR PUPPY NOT TO BITE

STEP 1	*Start by focusing on harder bites by monitoring the level of bite pressure during play time.*
STEP 2	*When your puppy bites a little too hard, loudly and emphatically say "OUCH!", playing up the pain level. Keep whatever your puppy is biting still and wait for your puppy to release it. Avoid pulling away.*
STEP 3	*When the biting stops, praise your puppy for stopping and redirect their biting to a chew toy.*
STEP 4	*Repeat steps 1-3 until your puppy starts biting you with very little pressure. Gradually repeat steps 1-3 with softer bites.*

TROUBLESHOOTING

- If your puppy goes quickly back to biting with equal intensity after you say "OUCH!", repeat the word "OUCH!" and leave the room. Your puppy will associate the "OUCH!" with a clear refusal to play, learning that if they bite too hard they play alone. After 30 seconds come back into the room with a chew toy and continue playing.

- If your puppy bites loose clothing say "OUCH!" and leave the room. Wait 30 seconds before returning and resuming play.

HELPFUL TIPS

- Puppies learn how to refrain from hard bites quite quickly but are unable to hold back on most other forms of play-biting early on. Bite inhibition relies on self-control which follows a puppy's developmental milestones. Intensity will decrease before frequency.

- Giving your puppy lots of play time with other puppies helps decrease the intensity and frequency of biting.

- Hand-feeding your puppy their meals can teach them to be gentler with their mouths. You can practice this by holding the kibble to the palm of your hand with your thumb. Say "Gentle" to your puppy as they try to eat the kibble but only release it when they are being gentle.

- Early on, avoid giving your puppy squeaky toys. They cause hyperactivity and encourage them to bite down hard while playing.

ISOLATION DISTRESS

A puppy who exhibits distress, usually in the form of barking or whining, when separated from their owner is experiencing isolation distress. If the behavior isn't addressed, it can develop into full blown separation anxiety which commonly leads to excessive barking, destructive chewing, drooling, panting, urinating, pacing, aggressiveness, and depression.

WHY WE TEACH PUPPIES TO ENJOY BEING ALONE

Puppies are extremely social animals and their strong preference is to be around others. Although this is nice for cuddle time on the couch, it's important for your puppy to value some alone time to avoid an unhealthy dependency and prevent isolation distress or separation anxiety from developing.

HOW TO TEACH YOUR PUPPY TO ENJOY BEING ALONE

STEP 1	Put your puppy in their crate, an expen, or their puppy room.
STEP 2	Give them a chew toy, a chew toy stuffed with treats, or a bone.
STEP 3	Wait quietly with them until they've settled down.
STEP 4	Quietly leave the room or, at a minimum, their line of sight for a minute or two.
STEP 5	Once the minute is up, return to them with a treat and sit with them quietly for a few more minutes before letting them out.
STEP 6	Gradually increase the length of time in step 4 until they are completely comfortable being alone.

TROUBLESHOOTING

- If your puppy starts whining or barking when you leave the room, hold off on going back in until they quiet down. On your next attempt, try reducing the length of time you are outside of the room to avoid reaching the stage where your puppy will bark or whine.

- If your puppy won't settle when you first put them in the crate, even with a stuffed chew toy or bone, refer back to the barking and whining section for additional guidance.

HELPFUL TIPS

- Offering your puppy interesting activities and high-value treats during their time alone gives them something to look forward to and distracts them from your absence.

A SPECIAL NOTE ABOUT CODDLING

Petting and showing your puppy affection is an important way to bond, and make them feel secure and loved. In excess, it can also be problematic. A lack of boundaries creates an unhealthy dependency that is stressful for your puppy, hard on their mental health, and can lead to isolation distress, separation anxiety or resource guarding behaviors. Be mindful of how much time you spend coddling your puppy.

ALONE TIME PROGRESS

WEEK	ALONE TIME HH:MM	PROGRESS
1		1 | 2 | 3 | 4 | 5
2		1 | 2 | 3 | 4 | 5
3		1 | 2 | 3 | 4 | 5
4		1 | 2 | 3 | 4 | 5
5		1 | 2 | 3 | 4 | 5
6		1 | 2 | 3 | 4 | 5
7		1 | 2 | 3 | 4 | 5
8		1 | 2 | 3 | 4 | 5

(1 = Not Comfortable Alone, 5 = Comfortable Alone)

NOTES

NAME RECOGNITION

WHY WE TEACH "NAME RECOGNITION"

Name recognition is an important training milestone; it conditions your puppy to value their name through reward association. Once this conditioning is firmly in place, your puppy will pay attention and show interest when their name is called, which makes future training milestones easier to accomplish.

HOW TO TEACH YOUR PUPPY THEIR NAME

STEP 1 — Say your puppy's name.

STEP 2 — When they turn in your direction or look at you give them a treat.

STEP 3 — You'll need to repeat this exercise on average 100 times over multiple training sessions.

HELPFUL TIPS

- Don't use your puppy's name when reprimanding - try "No" or "That's Enough" instead. Only use your puppy's name in a nice way when you are rewarding them, doing fun things together, or praising them.

MY PUPPY'S ENTHUSIASM LEVEL WHEN THEY HEAR THEIR NAME

TRAINING SESSION	PROGRESS
1	1 | 2 | 3 | 4 | 5
2	1 | 2 | 3 | 4 | 5
3	1 | 2 | 3 | 4 | 5
4	1 | 2 | 3 | 4 | 5
5	1 | 2 | 3 | 4 | 5
6	1 | 2 | 3 | 4 | 5
7	1 | 2 | 3 | 4 | 5
8	1 | 2 | 3 | 4 | 5

(1 = Not Enthusiastic, 5 = Very Enthusiastic)

MARK THE MOMENT

A key ingredient to successfully training basic obedience behaviors is letting your puppy know they've done a good job. To do this reliably requires conditioning your puppy to a word or sound that gets that message across. We call this "Marking the Moment". The word or sound you use can be anything. Throughout the remainder of this puppy training and raising program the "Mark the Moment" word is "Yes."

WHY WE TEACH "MARK THE MOMENT"

Treats are one way to let your puppy know they've done something right and reinforce behaviors. The problem with relying on treats alone to communicate this information is that it needs to be done immediately. On average, a puppy has a two-second window before they no longer associate the treat with the behavior you are trying to reward. Here's a common scenario:

> *Your puppy sits after receiving your "Sit" cue word. As you reach for a treat, your puppy begins sniffing the ground. By the time you reward your puppy with the treat, they associate the prize with their ground sniffing behavior instead of their compliance with your "Sit" command!*

By using a "Mark the Moment" word, you can immediately give your puppy feedback on a job well done. This reduces the likelihood of reinforcing the wrong behavior and makes teaching your puppy easier.

HOW TO TEACH "MARK THE MOMENT"

STEP 1 — Stand in front of your puppy with a treat in hand to get their attention. Hold the treat with your palm facing in and at chest level.

STEP 2 — Say "Yes."

STEP 3 — Swing the hand with the treat down toward the ground with your palm facing up and, as your puppy approaches, give them the treat. Make sure you say "Yes" before you start to swing your hand down.

STEP 4 — Quickly place another treat in your hand and repeat steps 1-3.

 "MARK THE MOMENT" WORD: YES
(positive feedback word)

TROUBLESHOOTING

🦴 If your puppy seems bored during this exercise and keeps wandering off to do other things, "reload" your hand with treats more quickly and don't stand still. Your puppy will find your movement motivating and will redirect their attention back to you.

🦴 If your puppy doesn't enthusiastically retrieve the treat once you've said "Yes" or looks at you confused, they haven't been fully conditioned to the word and you'll need to do more repetitions of the "Mark the Moment" exercise. It takes an average of 150 repetitions of the "Mark the Moment" exercise to condition your puppy to understand that "Yes" means "good job, you've earned a reward".

HELPFUL TIPS

🐾 "Yes" also acts to release your puppy from a behavior. It signals to them that the request to perform a behavior has been fulfilled and that they are 'done'.

🐾 An alternative to a "Mark the Moment" word is the use of a clicker sound (trainers call this "clicker training"). Tools known as 'clickers' are widely available for purchase and specifically designed for this purpose. Whether you use a clicker sound or a designated "Mark the Moment" word like "Yes" is purely preferential.

MY PUPPY'S ENTHUSIASM LEVEL WHEN THEY HEAR "YES"

WEEK	ENTHUSIASM
1	1 | 2 | 3 | 4 | 5
2	1 | 2 | 3 | 4 | 5

(1 = Not Enthusiastic, 5 = Very Enthusiastic)

NOTES

CORRECTIVE FEEDBACK

WHY WE TEACH "NO"

Just as it is important to communicate positive feedback, it's equally valuable to communicate undesirable behavior to reduce the odds of it being repeated. Without this feedback, your puppy will choose for themselves how to behave which rarely results in a well-behaved puppy!

HOW TO TEACH YOUR PUPPY "NO"

STEP 1	*When your puppy does something undesirable that can't be ignored because it is self-rewarding (chewing on your shoe for example), say "No" in a calm, firm, and assertive tone.*
STEP 2	*Your disapproving "No" should distract your puppy away from the undesirable behavior, at which point you can praise them for stopping and redirect their attention to a more desirable behavior.*
STEP 3	*If your puppy returns to the undesirable behavior, only pausing briefly when you say "No", put them in a short timeout. When timeout is over, redirect your puppy's attention to a more desirable behavior.*

 CORRECTIVE FEEDBACK WORD: NO

TROUBLESHOOTING

- 100% consistency in your use of "No" is the key to eliminating unwanted behaviors. If you let your puppy 'get away with it' from time to time, they will only learn that they can continue to behave as usual.

- Ignoring unwanted behaviors (that are not self-rewarding) can sometimes have the strongest impact. For example, the reward for your puppy jumping up on you is your attention. By ignoring the behavior and withholding attention until they have all four paws on the ground, you teach them the behavior needed to access the reward (your attention).

HELPFUL TIPS

- Only say "No" when you catch your puppy red handed and always say it in a calm, assertive tone.

- Remember to focus more on highlighting positive behaviors to your puppy through the use of "Yes", praise, and treats.

- When teaching basic obedience behaviors, don't use "No" as it hinders your puppy's learning process and creates a negative association with learning basic obedience. Instead, when training try saying something like "Nope" in a slightly upbeat voice and withhold rewards to let your puppy know they got something wrong.

🐾 GAMES 🐾
"FOLLOW THE LEADER" & "SEEK"

"FOLLOW THE LEADER"

"Follow the Leader" is a game where your puppy follows your hand closely with their nose.

WHY PLAY "FOLLOW THE LEADER"

"Follow the Leader" is a great way to teach your puppy the value of paying attention to your hands and nonverbal cues, which makes teaching your puppy common behaviors like "Sit" and "Down" much easier.

HOW TO PLAY

STEP 1	Show your puppy a treat and then use your thumb to pinch the treat to the palm of your hand.
STEP 2	Bring the palm of your hand very close to your puppy's nose and start walking (your puppy should be following your hand closely).
STEP 3	Periodically give your puppy the treat from your hand and replace it with a new one before continuing to walk.
STEP 4	Change how frequently you feed your puppy treats; adjust the direction and pace of your walk to keep your puppy engaged.

"SEEK"

"Seek" is a game where your puppy is asked to search for rewards.

WHY PLAY "SEEK"

Seek is a great way to tap into your puppy's hardwired instincts to search for, and find, food. Not only do they have a great time playing it, it also engages them in both mental and physical exercise.

HOW TO PLAY

STEP 1	*Show your puppy a treat.*
STEP 2	*Put your hands behind your back, place the treat in one hand, and make two fists.*
STEP 3	*Show your puppy both fists and say "Seek".*
STEP 4	*Open whichever fist your puppy touches first with their nose. If your puppy finds the treat, feed it to them. If not, show them your empty hand and repeat step 2 & 3.*
STEP 5	*Once your puppy is familiar with the game, try this variation - hide treats around your home while someone else is holding your puppy in place. Once the treats are all hidden, shout "Seek" and release your puppy to roam the house in search of the hidden treats.*

PUPPY TRAINING AND RAISING

WEEK TWO: GETTING TO KNOW EACH OTHER

INTRODUCTION

WHAT TO KNOW: PREPARING FOR THE WEEK AHEAD

Classical conditioning, which was first detailed in the Nobel Prize-winning research conducted by Ivan Pavlov in a series of experiments informally known today as 'Pavlov's Dogs', is a powerful learning process frequently used throughout this program. In week one, you used classical conditioning to create meaning and value behind "Yes", the "Mark the Moment" word. You also used it to create positive associations for your puppy with their crate and their socialization experiences. But be aware of the unintended classical conditioning lessons you teach your puppy which may cause them stress and anxiety. For example, if you leave the house every time you pick up your house keys, your puppy will develop an involuntary response to keys that causes them anxiety, stress and/or sadness. Be mindful of how these casual routines impact your newest member of the family.

TO-DO LIST

SECTIONS TO READ	DONE
Training Tips	☐
Luring and Verbal Cues	☐
Puppy Communication	☐
Leash Training	☐
Resource Guarding	☐
Lured Sit	☐
Lured Down	☐
Recall	☐

LEARNING OUTCOMES

The Focus of This Week Is On:

- Limiting the number of bathroom accidents your puppy has in a day.

- Introducing them to new people and other puppies.

- Teaching common behaviors like "Sit", "Down", and the "Recall".

- Teaching them that play-biting can hurt.

BY THE END OF THIS WEEK YOUR PUPPY SHOULD:

- *Have interacted with or seen 15-20 new people.*

- *Spend 5-10 minutes of alone time in their crate without whining and crying while you're at home.*

- *Be comfortable in their crate with the door shut for short periods of time and randomly go into their crate on their own.*

- *Be able to follow your daily routine - awake and ready to engage during playtime and sleepy at nap time.*

- *Be comfortable wearing a leash around the house.*

- *Show they understand your hand gestures for a "Lured Sit" by performing the behavior when you make the gesture.*

- *Make progress towards a "Lured Down" by trying to perform the behavior when you make the gesture.*

- *Run over to you enthusiastically when you say "Come".*

WEEK 2 CURRICULUM GETTING TO KNOW ❖ EACH OTHER ❖

10-MINUTE MORNING TRAINING SESSIONS

DAY 8	☐ Practice a "Lured Sit": 15 repetitions
DAY 9	☐ Practice a "Lured Sit": 15 repetitions
DAY 10	☐ Practice the "Recall": 10 repetitions ☐ Practice "Go to your Crate": 10 repetitions
DAY 11	☐ Practice "Go to your Crate": 10 repetitions ☐ Practice "Mark the Moment": 10 repetitions
DAY 12	☐ Practice a "Lured Down": 15 repetitions
DAY 13	☐ Practice a "Lured Down": 15 repetitions ☐ Practice "Go to your Crate": 10 repetitions ☐ Practice Leash Training
DAY 14	☐ Practice a "Lured Down": 15 repetitions ☐ Practice "Go to your Crate": 10 repetitions

GAMES TO INCORPORATE INTO PLAYTIME THIS WEEK

"Follow the Leader" | "Seek"

10-MINUTE AFTERNOON TRAINING SESSIONS

DAY 8	☐ Practice "Mark the Moment": 10 repetitions ☐ Practice a "Lured Sit": 15 repetitions
DAY 9	☐ Practice the "Recall": 10 repetitions
DAY 10	☐ Practice a "Lured Sit": 15 repetitions ☐ Practice "Go to your Crate": 10 repetitions
DAY 11	☐ Practice "Go to your Crate": 10 repetitions ☐ Practice the "Recall": 10 repetitions
DAY 12	☐ Practice a "Lured Down": 15 repetitions ☐ Practice Leash Training
DAY 13	☐ Practice "Go to your Crate": 10 repetitions ☐ Practice the "Recall": 10 repetitions
DAY 14	☐ Practice a "Lured Down": 15 repetitions ☐ Practice "Go to your Crate": 10 repetitions

FIELD TRIPS

- [ ] Sit at a coffee shop with your puppy on your lap.
- [ ] Attend a puppy socialization class.

SOCIALIZATION

- [ ] Brush and groom your puppy.
- [ ] Perform a handling routine.
- [ ] Cradle your puppy in your arms (like you would hold a newborn baby).
- [ ] Grab your puppy's collar and release it.
- [ ] Introduce your puppy to, or let them see, toddlers and young children.
- [ ] Introduce your puppy to, or let them see, a variety of men.
- [ ] Introduce your puppy to, or let them see, a variety of women.
- [ ] Have your puppy play with other vaccinated puppies who play well.
- [ ] Expose your puppy to city and traffic noises, including sirens.
- [ ] Play everyday sounds that will be a part of your puppy's life (traffic noises, babies crying, toddlers screaming, fireworks etc.) at a very low volume while they eat.

HELPFUL TIPS

- Clean up your puppy's accidents with an enzyme cleaner.
- Jumping up, yanking your hand, or yelling will excite your puppy and encourage them to bite more.
- It's best to train your puppy in a quiet place when they are hungry.
- Don't feed your puppy every meal in their bowl - use kibble as a reward in training sessions.
- Always stand next to your puppy when they are relieving themselves and ignore requests to play.
- Every interaction with your puppy is a training session; be aware of how you are rewarding and reinforcing different behaviors.
- Interactions between toddlers and young children must be supervised carefully – one bad encounter can create a lifelong aversion to children.

DEVELOPING GOOD DAILY HABITS

Use your housetraining verbal cue word and take your puppy to the exact same bathroom spot.	M | T | W | T | F | S | S ☐ ☐ ☐ ☐ ☐ ☐ ☐
Place treats in your puppy's crate at random times for them to find.	M | T | W | T | F | S | S ☐ ☐ ☐ ☐ ☐ ☐ ☐
Put your puppy in the crate with a treat-stuffed chew toy or bone (keeping the door open to start).	M | T | W | T | F | S | S ☐ ☐ ☐ ☐ ☐ ☐ ☐
Feed your puppy in the crate, keeping the door closed for a few more minutes once they finish eating.	M | T | W | T | F | S | S ☐ ☐ ☐ ☐ ☐ ☐ ☐
Periodically place a treat between your puppy's paws when they are calm and lying down.	M | T | W | T | F | S | S ☐ ☐ ☐ ☐ ☐ ☐ ☐
When leaving the house, do it quietly without a prolonged or emotional goodbye.	M | T | W | T | F | S | S ☐ ☐ ☐ ☐ ☐ ☐ ☐
Choose two meals this week to hand feed your puppy each piece of kibble by saying "Gentle" and releasing the food when your puppy obeys.	M | T | W | T | F | S | S ☐ ☐ ☐ ☐ ☐ ☐ ☐
Say "OUCH" loudly and emphatically to hard play-bites. Praise and redirect your puppy's biting to a chew toy.	M | T | W | T | F | S | S ☐ ☐ ☐ ☐ ☐ ☐ ☐
Put your puppy in their crate, exercise pen, or puppy room for some alone time and refer to the isolation distress section for creating positive alone experiences.	M | T | W | T | F | S | S ☐ ☐ ☐ ☐ ☐ ☐ ☐

BASIC OBEDIENCE TRAINING TIPS

- Carry treats at all times.

- Keep training sessions short – roughly five to ten minutes – twice daily.

- The best treats are small, soft, and fragrant.

- Engagement is the key to a great training session. Use movement and speed to keep your puppy focused. Keep your energy levels high, move constantly, and add an element of surprise by varying the number of treats your puppy gets when performing a task.

- You can't train a bored puppy (see note above).

- If your puppy doesn't respond to a verbal cue, revert back to using hand gestures (luring) to prompt the behavior for a few repetitions before trying a cue word again.

- It takes at least 100 repetitions for puppies to understand verbal cue words indoors and even more repetitions when learning outside.

- Remember to use your cue word before making any movements with your hands.

- If your puppy doesn't fully complete the behavior it's okay to reward them for making progress.

- Once your puppy reliably performs a behavior, switch to rewarding your puppy at random intervals instead of after every repetition.

MY PUPPY'S FAVORITE TRAINING TREATS

_____
_____
_____
_____
_____
_____
_____
_____
_____
_____
_____

🐾 LURING AND 🐾 VERBAL CUES

WHY WE USE LURING

Luring uses hand movement to get your puppy to follow any kind of physical directive. It is an effective way to foster obedience without the use of force. Luring helps you quickly establish behaviors that would otherwise take your puppy a long time to learn through physical manipulation or free shaping (waiting for your puppy to coincidentally perform the behavior and then rewarding them for it).

Food is most commonly used for luring but you can use anything your puppy will follow closely with their nose.

WHY WE USE VERBAL CUES

Puppies have a much easier time understanding a verbal cue once they have mastered the behavior itself through luring alone. That said, verbal cues are helpful to ensure that your puppy will still perform behaviors in situations where luring doesn't make sense or you can't use luring as a prompt (like when your puppy is too far to see your hands or your hands aren't free).

WHAT YOU CAN USE AS A VERBAL CUE

Assign any word you like as your verbal cue word for a specific behavior but be sure that every verbal cue is associated with a single action. Confusion can arise when the word "Down" is used both as a verbal cue word for your puppy to lay down and as an instruction to get off the furniture. **This program assigns words to each of the behaviors being taught but feel free to use different words if that is your preference.**

NOTES

PUPPY 🐾 COMMUNICATION 🐾

PUPPY BODY LANGUAGE

Your puppy's body language is the main way for them to express emotions and intentions, both to other animals and to people. It's their favorite way of "talking" to you!

WHY WE TEACH PUPPY COMMUNICATION

Understanding your puppy's body language helps you keep them safe and happy, and keeps their socialization experiences positive. Here are some physical indications of your puppy's emotional state:

SIGNS TO WATCH FOR

GREEN ZONE	**HAPPY PUPPY**	🐾 Loose body movements 🐾 Open mouth 🐾 No panting
YELLOW ZONE	**WARY PUPPY**	🐾 Licking lips (the puppy equivalent of thumb sucking) 🐾 Half-moon eyes (showing the whites of their eyes) 🐾 Closed mouth 🐾 Yawning 🐾 Turning away 🐾 Shaking coat
RED ZONE	**FEARFUL PUPPY**	🐾 Tries to get away and/or hide 🐾 Crouches 🐾 Growls

HELPFUL TIPS

🐾 When an interaction puts your puppy in the red zone, it's best to stop and remove your puppy from the situation.

🐾 If you see signs that your puppy is in the yellow zone, use judgment to determine if you can defuse the situation or if it's best to end the interaction.

🐾 When speaking to your puppy, tone is everything. Use an animated tone for praise and encouragement, a soothing tone to help calm your puppy, and a firm and direct tone to correct your puppy's bad behavior.

MY PUPPY IS IN THE GREEN ZONE WHEN:

_____
_____
_____
_____

MY PUPPY IS IN THE YELLOW ZONE WHEN:

_____
_____
_____
_____

MY PUPPY IS IN THE RED ZONE WHEN:

_____
_____
_____
_____

LEASH TRAINING

WHY WE LEASH TRAIN

Teaching your puppy to walk calmly beside you in public starts with teaching them to walk beside you in private. Taking a few weeks to practice loose leash walking at home will set you up for success when you are eventually able to walk your puppy in public.

HOW TO INTRODUCE THE LEASH

STEP 1	*Attach the leash to your puppy and let it drag on the ground for a few minutes.*
STEP 2	*Start walking slowly around your space, calling your puppy to join you. If your puppy is so distracted by the leash that they won't take more than a few steps with you, a few treats should take their mind off the leash. Repeat over multiple training sessions until your puppy is happily ignoring the leash as they walk beside you.*
STEP 3	*Hold the leash in one hand, keeping the hand closest to your puppy free to offer up treats every three steps. When you hand the treats over, do it by the side of your thigh. After a few training sessions, space out the treats to roughly every 10 steps.*

TROUBLESHOOTING

- If your puppy bites on or plays with their leash while walking together, stop. Hold the top of the leash firmly in one hand and slide the other hand down the length of the leash until it reaches your puppy's mouth; there should be no slack left. Say "Drop It" and wait patiently, keeping your body and hands still until your puppy releases the leash. As soon as they drop it, say "Yes", continue walking, and offer them a treat. This is common in the beginning but, as long as you are consistent, your puppy will learn that biting the leash makes the walk stop.

- If your puppy pulls the slack out of the leash, stop walking until there is enough slack in the line before you continue your walk.

HELPFUL TIPS

- Do this exercise in a safe enclosed space like a back yard, garage, or larger room in your house.

- Consider using a lightweight leash for toy dogs; regular leashes can be too heavy for them.

RESOURCE GUARDING

WHY WE PREVENT RESOURCE GUARDING

A puppy who snaps, growls, or generally seems to be defending something they value (food, toys, people, etc.) from other puppies, dogs or humans is resource guarding. This instinctive behavior is natural for puppies to display but can become problematic when a full grown dog threatens to bite anyone who jeopardizes a resource they value.

HOW TO HELP PREVENT RESOURCE GUARDING

STEP 1	*Always control your puppy's access to resources (food, treats, toys, access to you, family members, furniture, and your bed).*
STEP 2	*Condition your puppy to associate your presence near a resource as a positive thing, through the use of treats or other rewards.*
STEP 3	*Incorporate the exercises in this section into your daily routine. Throughout the puppy training and raising curriculum you will be prompted to repeat these activities in the "Developing Good Daily Habits" section each week.*

TROUBLESHOOTING

🦴 If at any point your puppy starts to growl, curl its lips up, stare intensely at you, or show any other signs of aggression during the exercises provided, stop immediately and contact a professional trainer for further guidance.

HELPFUL TIPS

🐾 Watch your puppy's body language closely while you are performing these exercises for any signs of aggression.

🐾 Do not let young children perform these exercises.

EXERCISES

- [ ] Hand-feed your puppy each piece of kibble for a few meals each week.
- [ ] Approach your puppy while they are eating, drop a treat into their bowl, and walk away.
- [ ] Stand by your puppy's bowl and drop treats in while they are eating.
- [ ] While your puppy is eating, pick up the bowl about 1 to 2 feet off the ground and, while your puppy watches, place a treat in the bowl before returning it to the floor.
- [ ] Don't leave toys lying around the house, put them away when your puppy has finished playing with them.
- [ ] Exchange a toy your puppy is playing with for a high-value treat (cooked chicken for example) and give the toy back once they've finished eating.
- [ ] Don't let your puppy jump onto furniture without permission.

🐾 LURED SIT 🐾

WHY WE TEACH A "LURED SIT"

A "Lured Sit" teaches your puppy to sit when prompted by a hand gesture. Starting with this approach to "sit" training before introducing verbal cues helps solidify the behavior before creating a word association.

HOW TO LURE YOUR PUPPY INTO A "SIT"

STEP 1	*Clasping a treat in the palm of your hand with your thumb, bring your hand very close to your puppy's nose so they can smell the treat.*
STEP 2	*When your hand is almost touching their nose, raise it in an upward motion toward you (not over the back of your puppy's head), slowly enough that your puppy can follow it with ease.*
STEP 3	*Once your hand is high enough, your puppy will instinctively go into a seated position. When this happens say "Yes" and reward them with a treat.*
STEP 4	*When your puppy is reliably and enthusiastically sitting using a lure, wait for 5-10 seconds before saying "Yes". While waiting to 'release them' from the behavior, say "Good" and hand them a treat, followed by another "Good" and a second treat while they remain seated. After the time is up, say "Yes" to release your puppy from the sit position and offer a final treat.*

TROUBLESHOOTING

🦴 If your puppy doesn't move into a seated position, try reducing the distance between your hand and their nose and move your hand slower when making the upward motion.

🦴 If your puppy paws or bites at your hand when you move the treat over their head, say "Nope" and move the treat out of sight by placing your hands behind your back. Wait calmly for your puppy to settle down before trying again.

HELPFUL TIPS

🐾 By introducing the word "Good", you are telling your puppy "keep going, stay in position". It encourages your puppy to hold a position longer before saying "Yes", which releases them from the behavior.

🐾 Once your puppy is consistently performing a "Lured Sit", reduce the frequency of treats from every repetition down to occasionally offering a reward.

LURED SIT PROGRESS

WEEK	PROGRESS
2	1 | 2 | 3 | 4 | 5
3	1 | 2 | 3 | 4 | 5
4	1 | 2 | 3 | 4 | 5

(1 = Learning, 5 = Perfected)

LURED DOWN

WHY WE TEACH A "LURED DOWN"

A "Lured Down" teaches your puppy to lie down when prompted by a hand gesture. Starting with this approach to "down" training before introducing verbal cues helps solidify the behavior before creating a word association.

HOW TO LURE YOUR PUPPY INTO A "DOWN"

METHOD 1

STEP 1	*Clasp a treat in the palm of one hand with your thumb and place that hand into the other, positioning them out in front of you with your palms facing up. Then, with your hands still together, bring them very close to your puppy's nose to smell the treat.*
STEP 2	*Keeping your hands level in front of your puppy's nose, take a step toward your puppy while slowly lowering your hands toward the ground.*
STEP 3	*As soon as your puppy lies down say "Yes" and reward them with a treat.*
STEP 4	*When your puppy is reliably and enthusiastically lying down using a lure, wait for 5-10 seconds before saying "Yes". While waiting to 'release them' from the behavior, say "Good" and hand them a treat, followed by another "Good" and a second treat while they continue lying down. After the time is up, say "Yes" to release your puppy from the "down" position and offer a final treat.*

METHOD 2

STEP 1	*Lure your puppy into a sit position.*
STEP 2	*While still holding the treat, move your hand slowly down from your puppy's nose to their paws.*
STEP 3	*Slowly move your hand along the floor until your puppy lies down. Say "Yes" and reward them with a treat.*
STEP 4	*When your puppy is reliably and enthusiastically lying down using a lure, wait for 5-10 seconds before saying "Yes". While waiting to 'release them' from the behavior, say "Good" and hand them a treat, followed by another "Good" and a second treat while they continue lying down. After the time is up, say "Yes" to release your puppy from the "down" position and offer a final treat.*

TROUBLESHOOTING

- If your puppy struggles to get all four legs on the ground, start by rewarding them for any progress (a slight hunch, front elbows on the ground, etc).

- If you are luring your puppy into a down using method one and their rear end stays up, make sure you are keeping your hands level with your puppy's nose, not below it.

- If your puppy continues to have their rear end in the air, be patient and try waiting a little longer before rewarding them with a progress treat. Often, a bit of extra time encourages them to drop their hind legs to the ground.

HELPFUL TIPS

- By introducing the word "Good", you are telling your puppy "keep going, stay in position". It encourages your puppy to hold a position longer before saying "Yes", which releases them from the behavior.

- Once your puppy is consistently performing a "Lured Down", reduce the frequency of treats from every repetition down to occasionally offering a reward.

LURED DOWN PROGRESS

WEEK	PROGRESS
2	1 | 2 | 3 | 4 | 5
3	1 | 2 | 3 | 4 | 5
4	1 | 2 | 3 | 4 | 5

(1 = Learning, 5 = Perfected)

NOTES

RECALL

WHY WE TEACH A "RECALL"

A "Recall" behavior teaches your puppy to come over to you. When mastered, it frees your puppy to enjoy safe, off-leash time outside. Puppies who don't learn a "Recall" may always have to stay on leash.

HOW TO TEACH YOUR PUPPY TO RECALL

METHOD 1

STEP 1	*Have a helper hold your puppy's harness while you back away.*
STEP 2	*Say "Come" when you are about 10-15 feet away. Upon hearing you say "Come", the helper releases the harness. When your puppy commits to running toward you, say "Yes".*
STEP 3	*Continue to walk backward while your puppy is approaching you.*
STEP 4	*Shower your puppy with enthusiastic praise and a few treats as soon as they reach you.*

METHOD 2

STEP 1	*Enthusiastically say your puppy's name. Once you have their attention, say "Come" in an equally enthusiastic tone and start walking backwards.*
STEP 2	*As your puppy starts to move towards you say "Yes" and reward them with a treat and praise when they reach you.*

HOW TO TEACH YOUR PUPPY TO SAFELY RECALL OUTSIDE

STEP 1	*Leash your puppy using a 30ft long line leash.*
STEP 2	*Allow your puppy to wander away from you.*
STEP 3	*When your puppy nears the end of the leash, say "Come" and give the leash a quick tug.*
STEP 4	*As soon as your puppy turns to look at you, say "Yes" and start walking backward.*
STEP 5	*Continue backing up until your puppy catches you.*
STEP 6	*Praise and reward your puppy with a few treats when they reach you.*

 VERBAL CUE WORD: "COME"

TROUBLESHOOTING

- If your puppy was performing a recall behavior really well and has more recently stopped listening to your verbal cue, it may be because you've been using it exclusively in a negative context (ending play sessions, walks, and so on). Focus on re-creating positive associations for recall behaviors.

HELPFUL TIPS

- You'll have better success teaching your puppy a "Recall" in a setting with very few distractions.

- Games such as "Catch Me if You Can", "Guess Who", and "Hide and Go Seek" are a fun way to reinforce the "Recall" behavior.

- Don't train your puppy to recall in public places until they've received their full set of initial vaccinations and are protected from infectious diseases.

- Some dog breeds can never be trusted off leash due to their strong instinct to follow a scent or go after prey.

RECALL PROGRESS

WEEK	PROGRESS
2	1 | 2 | 3 | 4 | 5
3	1 | 2 | 3 | 4 | 5
4	1 | 2 | 3 | 4 | 5
5	1 | 2 | 3 | 4 | 5
6	1 | 2 | 3 | 4 | 5
7	1 | 2 | 3 | 4 | 5
8	1 | 2 | 3 | 4 | 5

(1 = Learning, 5 = Perfected)

OUTSIDE RECALL PROGRESS

WEEK	PROGRESS
8	1 | 2 | 3 | 4 | 5

(1 = Learning, 5 = Perfected)

WEEK THREE: SETTLING IN

INTRODUCTION

WHAT TO KNOW: PREPARING FOR THE WEEK AHEAD

With a consistent daily routine now in place, your puppy will be settled into your home life. Your puppy is gaining confidence and may become more insistent and pushy when trying to get what they want. Remember that your puppy will repeat behaviors that prove successful in getting them what they want. If barking gets you to give them more attention - be it petting or even telling them "no" - they will continue to bark. Puppies are smart and you can count on them to find the approach that yields the best results!

TO-DO LIST

SECTIONS TO READ	DONE
Jumping Up	☐
Stay	☐
Touch	☐
Games: "Catch Me if You Can" & "Fetch"	☐

LEARNING OUTCOMES

The Focus of This Week Is On:

- 🐾 Building your puppy's confidence through ongoing socialization experiences.
- 🐾 Practicing "Lured Sit" and "Lured Down".
- 🐾 Introducing two new behaviors - "Touch" and "Stay".
- 🐾 Ensuring your puppy is happy spending time alone in their crate while you're at home.

BY THE END OF THIS WEEK YOUR PUPPY SHOULD:

- ⊘ *Have interacted with or seen 15-20 new people.*
- ⊘ *Spend 10-15 minutes of alone time in their crate without whining and crying while you're at home.*
- ⊘ *Be comfortable and relaxed while being brushed and handled.*
- ⊘ *Reduce the frequency of hard play-bites when playing.*
- ⊘ *Reliably perform a "Lured Sit" when asked.*
- ⊘ *Show they understand your hand gestures for a "Lured Down" by performing the behavior when you make the gesture.*
- ⊘ *Understand the concept of a "Stay" behavior by waiting for a brief period when you are a few steps away.*
- ⊘ *Understand the concept of a "Touch" behavior by touching the palm of your hand when you place it less than a foot away.*

WEEK 3 CURRICULUM
❖ SETTLING IN ❖

10-MINUTE MORNING TRAINING SESSIONS

DAY 15	☐ Practice a "Lured Down": 15 repetitions ☐ Practice "Touch": 10 repetitions
DAY 16	☐ Practice "Go to your Crate": 10 repetitions ☐ Practice "Touch": 10 repetitions ☐ Practice Leash Training
DAY 17	☐ Practice a "Lured Down": 15 repetitions ☐ Practice Leash Training
DAY 18	☐ Practice "Stay": 10 repetitions
DAY 19	☐ Practice a "Lured Sit": 15 repetitions
DAY 20	☐ Practice the "Recall": 10 repetitions
DAY 21	☐ Practice the "Recall": 10 repetitions

GAMES TO INCORPORATE INTO PLAYTIME THIS WEEK

"Catch Me If You Can" | "Fetch"

10-MINUTE AFTERNOON TRAINING SESSIONS

DAY 15	☐ Practice a "Lured Down": 15 repetitions ☐ Practice "Go to your Crate": 10 repetitions
DAY 16	☐ Practice a "Lured Sit": 15 repetitions
DAY 17	☐ Practice "Touch": 10 repetitions ☐ Practice the "Recall": 10 repetitions
DAY 18	☐ Practice "Stay": 10 repetitions
DAY 19	☐ Practice a "Lured Down": 15 repetitions ☐ Practice "Go to your Crate": 10 repetitions
DAY 20	☐ Practice "Stay": 10 repetitions ☐ Practice "Touch": 10 repetitions
DAY 21	☐ Practice "Stay": 10 repetitions ☐ Practice Leash Training

FIELD TRIPS

- [ ] Sit on a bench with your puppy on your lap.
- [ ] Take your puppy to a friend's house.

SOCIALIZATION

- [ ] Brush and groom your puppy.
- [ ] Perform a handling routine.
- [ ] Grab your puppy's collar and release it.
- [ ] Brush your puppy's teeth.
- [ ] Introduce your puppy to, or let them see, elderly people.
- [ ] Introduce your puppy to, or let them see, people of different ethnicities.
- [ ] Have your puppy play with other vaccinated puppies who play well.
- [ ] Expose your puppy to umbrellas, strollers, and shopping carts.
- [ ] Expose your puppy to runners and cyclists.
- [ ] Play everyday sounds that will be a part of your puppy's life (traffic noises, babies crying, toddlers screaming, fireworks etc.) at a very low volume while they eat.

HELPFUL TIPS

- 🐾 Don't play with your puppy or train them in the area of the house where you primarily want them to settle and be quiet.
- 🐾 Mental stimulation from training and games is just as tiring for your puppy as physical exercise.
- 🐾 If your puppy shows excitement while waiting for their food bowl, wait until they have calmed down before you place it on the ground. This helps them develop self-control.
- 🐾 When it comes to unwanted behaviors, expect a decrease in intensity before you see a decrease in frequency.

DEVELOPING GOOD DAILY HABITS

Use your housetraining verbal cue word and take your puppy to the exact same bathroom spot.	M │ T │ W │ T │ F │ S │ S ☐ ☐ ☐ ☐ ☐ ☐ ☐
Feed your puppy in the crate, keeping the door closed for a few more minutes once they finish eating.	M │ T │ W │ T │ F │ S │ S ☐ ☐ ☐ ☐ ☐ ☐ ☐
Ignore your puppy when they whine and bark for your attention.	M │ T │ W │ T │ F │ S │ S ☐ ☐ ☐ ☐ ☐ ☐ ☐
Prepare a chew toy stuffed with treats or have a bone available for your puppy when you want them to settle and be quiet for a longer stretch of time.	M │ T │ W │ T │ F │ S │ S ☐ ☐ ☐ ☐ ☐ ☐ ☐
When you come home and your puppy greets you, wait for any jumping to stop and all four paws are on the ground before petting them.	M │ T │ W │ T │ F │ S │ S ☐ ☐ ☐ ☐ ☐ ☐ ☐
Choose two meals this week to hand feed your puppy each piece of kibble by saying "Gentle" and releasing the food when your puppy obeys.	M │ T │ W │ T │ F │ S │ S ☐ ☐ ☐ ☐ ☐ ☐ ☐
Say "OUCH" loudly and emphatically to hard play-bites. Praise and redirect your puppy's biting to a chew toy.	M │ T │ W │ T │ F │ S │ S ☐ ☐ ☐ ☐ ☐ ☐ ☐
Put your puppy in their crate, exercise pen, or puppy room for some alone time and refer to the isolation distress section for creating positive alone experiences.	M │ T │ W │ T │ F │ S │ S ☐ ☐ ☐ ☐ ☐ ☐ ☐

JUMPING UP

WHY WE TEACH PUPPIES NOT TO JUMP

Puppies will instinctively jump up to greet people. Training your puppy to greet people with all four paws on the ground means you don't have to worry about visitors getting knocked over when you open the front door, and fewer dirty paw prints on your clothes when you get home for work.

HOW TO TEACH YOUR PUPPY NOT TO JUMP

METHOD 1

STEP 1	Have treats with you when you come home.
STEP 2	If your puppy attempts to greet you by jumping up, silently ignore them and move your body away to avoid the jump.
STEP 3	When your puppy tires from jumping and returns their four paws to the ground, feed them a treat and give them praise.

METHOD 2

STEP 1	Place a leash on your puppy and, while holding the leash, lure them with a treat toward the guest they are interested in greeting.
STEP 2	As you approach the guest, instruct your puppy to "Say Hello" by luring them into a "Sit".
STEP 3	With your puppy seated, invite your guest to pet your puppy while you say "Good". After a few more moments, say "Yes" and give your puppy a treat.

TROUBLESHOOTING

🦴 If your puppy continues to jump, it may be due to a lack of consistency following the methods outlined every time someone enters the house.

HELPFUL TIPS

🐾 Once your puppy has learned the "Touch" behavior, you can use it as a greeting. Instead of jumping up to greet guests, they will touch the palm of their hand – the equivalent of a doggie handshake!

JUMPING PROGRESS

WEEK	PROGRESS
3	1　|　2　|　3　|　4　|　5
4	1　|　2　|　3　|　4　|　5
5	1　|　2　|　3　|　4　|　5
6	1　|　2　|　3　|　4　|　5
7	1　|　2　|　3　|　4　|　5
8	1　|　2　|　3　|　4　|　5

(1 = Learning, 5 = Perfected)

STAY

WHY WE TEACH "STAY"

A "Stay" behavior teaches your puppy to hold a position for an undefined length of time. Typically a "Stay" is paired with the "Sit" position, but your puppy doesn't necessarily need to be seated. A "Stay" behavior is very useful for teaching your puppy self-control and, in some cases, protects them from unsafe situations.

HOW TO TEACH YOUR PUPPY "STAY"

STEP 1	Ask and/or lure your puppy into a sit position with a treat in one hand.
STEP 2	Say "Stay", and using your free hand make a stopping gesture.
STEP 3	Take one or two steps back and pause for three seconds.
STEP 4	If your puppy stays seated, say "Yes" and reward them a treat. If they move, say "Nope" and go back to step 1.
STEP 5	Gradually increase the number of steps you take, and the length of time you pause, before saying "Yes" to release them from the stay behavior.

 VERBAL CUE WORD: "STAY"

TROUBLESHOOTING

🦴 If your puppy is struggling to "Stay", make the exercise easier by taking fewer steps back and rewarding them quicker. As your puppy's response improves, you can progressively increase the difficulty.

HELPFUL TIPS

🐾 It's always best to teach this behavior in a quiet, distraction-free, environment.

🐾 Asking your puppy to "Sit" and "Stay" before you give them things they want like a meal. This teaches them manners - the equivalent of saying 'please' when asking for something.

"STAY" PROGRESS

WEEK	PROGRESS	DURATION	DISTANCE
3	1 | 2 | 3 | 4 | 5		
4	1 | 2 | 3 | 4 | 5		
5	1 | 2 | 3 | 4 | 5		
6	1 | 2 | 3 | 4 | 5		
7	1 | 2 | 3 | 4 | 5		
8	1 | 2 | 3 | 4 | 5		

(1 = Learning, 5 = Perfected)

TOUCH

WHY WE TEACH "TOUCH"

A "Touch" behavior signals to your puppy to touch something with their nose. It's a valuable and versatile skill that can be used in a number of ways. It can be used as a greeting, in lieu of a "Recall" behavior, as a way to redirect your puppy's attention to you, and even as a means to teach your puppy to close doors or flip a light switch!

HOW TO TEACH YOUR PUPPY "TOUCH"

STEP 1	Bring your open palm very close to your puppy's nose.
STEP 2	Say "Touch" and, when your puppy touches your palm with their nose, say "Yes" and reward them with a treat.
STEP 3	Raise the difficulty. As your puppy gets better at step 2, continue to make the exercise challenging by gradually increasing the distance between your palm and your puppy's nose.

 VERBAL CUE WORD: "TOUCH"

TROUBLESHOOTING

🦴 Puppies generally pick up on this behavior very quickly but, if your puppy struggles, bring your palm closer to your puppy's nose and say "Yes", rewarding them with a treat if they make any kind of movement toward your palm.

"TOUCH" PROGRESS

WEEK	PROGRESS
3	1 | 2 | 3 | 4 | 5
4	1 | 2 | 3 | 4 | 5
5	1 | 2 | 3 | 4 | 5
6	1 | 2 | 3 | 4 | 5
7	1 | 2 | 3 | 4 | 5
8	1 | 2 | 3 | 4 | 5

(1 = Learning, 5 = Perfected)

🐾 GAMES 🐾
"CATCH ME IF YOU CAN" & "FETCH"

"CATCH ME IF YOU CAN"

"Catch Me If You Can" is a game where your puppy is asked to seek out and find a person.

WHY PLAY "CATCH ME IF YOU CAN"

"Catch Me if You Can" is a great way to reinforce the "Recall" behavior while teaching your puppy the names of family members and friends.

STEP 1	Have a helper hold your puppy while you show them a treat or their favorite toy.
STEP 2	While your puppy is watching, move quickly and find somewhere to hide in your home.
STEP 3	Once you're hidden, the helper holding your puppy shouts "Find [Your Name]!" and releases them to search for you.
STEP 4	When you've been found, feed your puppy a treat or give them a favorite toy to play with.

"FETCH"

"Fetch" is a game where you throw an object a short distance for your puppy to retrieve.

WHY PLAY "FETCH"

"Fetch" is a great way to exercise and bond with your puppy.

STEP 1	*Pick an object (e.g. a toy) for your puppy to fetch. Introduce the object to your puppy by placing it on the ground and, when they show interest in it or touch it, say "Yes" and reward them with a treat. Repeat this process until your puppy is excited to have the object.*
STEP 2	*Move the object around so your puppy has to move to get to it. Don't throw the object yet, simply place it in different spots near you. Each time they touch the object, say "Yes" and reward them with a treat.*
STEP 3	*Repeat step 2 but this time only say "Yes" when they lift the object with their mouth.*
STEP 4	*Say "Fetch" and throw the object about 5 feet, and when your puppy runs to get it encourage them to bring it back. Do this by taking a few steps back and saying "Yes" when they start to move toward you. Offer your puppy a treat when they reach you, pick up the object, and repeat.*

TROUBLESHOOTING

🦴 If your puppy doesn't come back to you after retrieving the toy, put them on a 6-foot leash until they learn to come back consistently.

HELPFUL TIPS

🐾 It's helpful to use your puppy's favorite toy when playing this game.

WEEK FOUR: MANNERS PLEASE

INTRODUCTION

WHAT TO KNOW:
PREPARING FOR THE WEEK AHEAD

Your puppy is a big ball of energy that needs to learn productive ways to expend and control that excitement. Fortunately, with a little help from you, your puppy will quickly learn how to control themselves and their behavior. You'll be amazed by how much self-control your puppy can develop by consistently asking them to perform behaviors before rewarding them with things like dinner, walks, and playtime!

TO-DO LIST

SECTIONS TO READ	DONE
Sit	☐
Down	☐

LEARNING OUTCOMES

The Focus of This Week Is On:

- Introducing your puppy to verbal cues for the most frequently requested behaviors: "Sit" and "Down".
- Practicing the "Stay", "Recall" and "Touch" behaviors.
- Making your puppy work for rewards like treats, meals, and toys.
- Ignoring your puppy when they bark or jump up for attention.

BY THE END OF THIS WEEK YOUR PUPPY SHOULD:

- ☑ *Have interacted with or seen 15-20 new people.*
- ☑ *Spend 15-20 minutes of alone time in their crate without whining and crying while you're at home.*
- ☑ *Reliably go to the bathroom in the designated area.*
- ☑ *Not shy away or duck when you grab their collar.*
- ☑ *Not bite or chew on their leash.*
- ☑ *Be relaxed and calm when hearing regular household noises.*
- ☑ *Be comfortable and relaxed spending time, both asleep and awake, in their crate.*
- ☑ *Consistently perform a "Recall" behavior in a training environment with few distractions (still may not work 100% of the time).*
- ☑ *Reliably remain in a "Stay" behavior for no less than 5 seconds while you move 3 feet away.*
- ☑ *Reliably perform a "Touch" behavior when you are standing no less than 3 feet away.*
- ☑ *Reliably perform a "Lured Down" when asked.*

WEEK 4 CURRICULUM
❖ MANNERS PLEASE ❖

10-MINUTE MORNING TRAINING SESSIONS

DAY 22	☐ Practice "Sit": 15 repetitions ☐ Practice "Go to your Crate": 10 repetitions
DAY 23	☐ Practice "Stay": 10 repetitions ☐ Practice "Go to your Crate": 10 repetitions
DAY 24	☐ Practice a "Lured Down": 15 repetitions ☐ Practice "Sit": 15 repetitions
DAY 25	☐ Practice "Sit": 15 repetitions ☐ Practice "Stay": 10 repetitions
DAY 26	☐ Practice the "Recall": 10 repetitions
DAY 27	☐ Practice "Sit": 15 repetitions ☐ Practice "Stay": 10 repetitions
DAY 28	☐ Practice "Down": 15 repetitions

GAMES TO INCORPORATE INTO PLAYTIME THIS WEEK

"Catch Me If You Can" | "Fetch"

10-MINUTE AFTERNOON TRAINING SESSIONS

DAY 22
- [ ] Practice a "Lured Down": 15 repetitions
- [ ] Practice Leash Training

DAY 23
- [ ] Practice a "Lured Down": 15 repetitions

DAY 24
- [ ] Practice the "Recall": 10 repetitions
- [ ] Practice "Touch": 10 repetitions

DAY 25
- [ ] Practice "Down": 15 repetitions
- [ ] Practice "Touch": 10 repetitions

DAY 26
- [ ] Practice "Down": 15 repetitions

DAY 27
- [ ] Practice "Down": 15 repetitions

DAY 28
- [ ] Practice "Stay": 10 repetitions
- [ ] Practice Leash Training

FIELD TRIPS

- [ ] Sit at a busy coffee shop with your puppy on your lap.
- [ ] Take your puppy on two car rides (one at night).

SOCIALIZATION

- [ ] Grab your puppy's collar and release it.
- [ ] Gently squeeze your puppy's paws and trim or dremel their nails (pretend if they don't need their nails trimmed).
- [ ] Perform a handling routine.
- [ ] Introduce your puppy to, or let them see, toddlers and young children.
- [ ] Introduce your puppy to, or let them see, people with disabilities.
- [ ] Introduce your puppy to, or let them see, teenagers.
- [ ] Introduce your puppy to, or let them see, people wearing hats, backpacks and sunglasses.
- [ ] Have your puppy play with other vaccinated puppies who play well.
- [ ] Walk or place your puppy on a metal surface.
- [ ] Play everyday sounds that will be a part of your puppy's life (traffic noises, babies crying, toddlers screaming, fireworks etc.) at a very low volume while they eat.

HELPFUL TIPS

- 🐾 Getting your puppy to sit before rewarding them with food, toys, or an outing helps develop their self-control and improves their manners.
- 🐾 Remember to say your verbal cue words before you make any movements with your hands.
- 🐾 Having a few treats in your pocket keeps you ready to reward any good behavior you observe.

DEVELOPING GOOD DAILY HABITS

Habit	M	T	W	T	F	S	S
Ignore your puppy when they whine and bark for your attention.	☐	☐	☐	☐	☐	☐	☐
Prepare a chew toy stuffed with treats or have a bone available for your puppy when you want them to settle and be quiet for a longer stretch of time.	☐	☐	☐	☐	☐	☐	☐
Say "Crate" before you put your puppy in their crate.	☐	☐	☐	☐	☐	☐	☐
Ask your puppy to "Sit" before you feed them at breakfast and dinner.	☐	☐	☐	☐	☐	☐	☐
Stand by your puppy and drop treats in their bowl while they eat either breakfast or dinner.	☐	☐	☐	☐	☐	☐	☐
When you come home and your puppy greets you, wait for any jumping to stop and all four paws are on the ground before petting them.	☐	☐	☐	☐	☐	☐	☐
Say "OUCH" loudly and emphatically to hard play-bites. Praise and redirect your puppy's biting to a chew toy.	☐	☐	☐	☐	☐	☐	☐
Put your puppy in their crate, exercise pen, or puppy room for some alone time and refer to the isolation distress section for creating positive alone experiences.	☐	☐	☐	☐	☐	☐	☐

SIT

WHY WE TEACH "SIT"

"Sit" is a basic behavior that every puppy should know. It's a useful way to settle your puppy and calm them, and is also used as a foundation for learning more complex behaviors.

HOW TO TEACH YOUR PUPPY A "SIT" VERBAL CUE

STEP 1	*Say "Sit".*
STEP 2	*Lure your puppy into a sitting position.*
STEP 3	*As soon as your puppy sits, say "Yes" and reward them with a treat. Practice multiple repetitions of steps 1-3 across training seasons.*
STEP 4	*When your puppy starts sitting before you lure them into position, you can stop using the lure. Your puppy has now created an association between "Sit" and the behavior itself.*
STEP 5	*When your puppy is reliably and enthusiastically sitting on command, wait 5-10 seconds before saying "Yes". While waiting to 'release them' from the behavior, say "Good" and hand them a treat, followed by another "Good" and a second treat while they continue sitting. After the time is up, say "Yes" to release your puppy from the "Sit" position and offer a final treat.*

 VERBAL CUE WORD: "SIT"

TROUBLESHOOTING

🦴 Make sure you say your verbal cue word ahead of when you start luring your puppy into the sit position. Saying your verbal cue while moving your hand to lure your puppy will keep your puppy focused on the lure and not the word.

HELPFUL TIPS

🐾 When you start teaching your puppy a "Sit" behavior in a new environment you may have to briefly go back to using a lure.

🐾 Once your puppy is consistently performing a "Sit", reduce the frequency of treats from every repetition down to occasionally offering a reward.

"SIT" PROGRESS

WEEK	PROGRESS
4	1 | 2 | 3 | 4 | 5
5	1 | 2 | 3 | 4 | 5
6	1 | 2 | 3 | 4 | 5
7	1 | 2 | 3 | 4 | 5
8	1 | 2 | 3 | 4 | 5

(1 = Learning, 5 = Perfected)

DOWN

WHY WE TEACH "DOWN"

The "Down" behavior - where your puppy lays down on the ground - is a basic command that every dog should know. It's useful to help your puppy settle and relax in their most comfortable position.

HOW TO TEACH YOUR PUPPY A "DOWN" VERBAL CUE

STEP 1	Say "Down".
STEP 2	Lure your puppy into the lying down position.
STEP 3	As soon as your puppy lies down, say "Yes" and reward them with a treat. Practice multiple repetitions of steps 1-3 across training seasons.
STEP 4	When your puppy starts lying down before you lure them into position, you can stop using the lure. Your puppy has now created an association between "Down" and the behavior itself.
STEP 5	When your puppy is reliably and enthusiastically lying down on command, wait 5-10 seconds before saying "Yes". While waiting to 'release them' from the behavior, say "Good" and hand them a treat, followed by another "Good" and a second treat while they continue to stay down. After the time is up, say "Yes" to release your puppy from the "Down" position and offer a final treat.

 VERBAL CUE WORD: "DOWN"

TROUBLESHOOTING

🦴 Make sure you say your verbal cue word ahead of when you start luring your puppy into the down position. Saying your verbal cue while moving your hand to lure your puppy will keep your puppy focused on the lure and not the word.

HELPFUL TIPS

🐾 When you start teaching your puppy a "Down" behavior in a new environment you may have to briefly go back to using a lure.

🐾 Once your puppy is consistently performing a "Down", reduce the frequency of treats from every repetition down to occasionally offering a reward.

"DOWN" PROGRESS

WEEK	PROGRESS
4	1 | 2 | 3 | 4 | 5
5	1 | 2 | 3 | 4 | 5
6	1 | 2 | 3 | 4 | 5
7	1 | 2 | 3 | 4 | 5
8	1 | 2 | 3 | 4 | 5

(1 = Learning, 5 = Perfected)

SECOND MONTH AT A GLANCE

DAY 29 **Behavior Intro:** Drop It	DAY 30 **Behavior Intro:** Leave It
DAY 33	DAY 34 **New Game:** Red Light, Green Light
DAY 37	DAY 38
DAY 41	DAY 42
DAY 45	DAY 46 **New Game:** Guess Who
DAY 49 **Evaluating Behaviors Test:** Recall	DAY 50 **Behavior Intro:** Loose Leash Walking
DAY 53 **Behavior Intro:** Name Redirection	DAY 54

DAY 31 **New Game:** Tug-of-War	**DAY 32** **Topic:** Chewing
DAY 35	**DAY 36** **BRINGING IT ALL TOGETHER:** **DAILY PRACTICE OF BEHAVIORS** ———————→
DAY 39	**DAY 40** ————————————→
DAY 43 **Topic:** Proofing	Evaluating Behaviors	**DAY 44** **New Game:** Hide and Go Seek
DAY 47 **Evaluating Behaviors Test:** Stay	**DAY 48** **Evaluating Behaviors Test:** Sit and Down
DAY 51	**DAY 52** **Behavior Intro:** Recall Outside on a Long Line
DAY 55 **8 WEEK PUPPY REPORT CARD**	**DAY 56** Your puppy has met or seen 100 new people	Congratulations!! Puppy Training and Raising Program Graduation

PUPPY TRAINING AND RAISING

WEEK FIVE: NOT EVEN THE DRYWALL IS SAFE

INTRODUCTION

WHAT TO KNOW:
PREPARING FOR THE WEEK AHEAD

Your puppy's adult teeth will begin to come in and sore gums for the next three months brings on a heightened desire to chew. Developmentally, your puppy will also have more energy now and, together, these two forces can wreak havoc in the house. Shoes, baseboards, couch cushions, and even drywall might make their way onto the chewing menu. Save your furniture by redirecting that energy into more positive distractions - training, games, toy puzzles and chew toys stuffed with treats are all great substitutes.

TO-DO LIST

SECTIONS TO READ	DONE
Chewing	☐
Leave It	☐
Drop It	☐
Games: "Tug-of-War" & "Red Light, Green Light"	☐

LEARNING OUTCOMES

The Focus of This Week Is On:

- Practicing the "Sit", "Down", "Stay", "Recall", and "Touch" behaviors to maintain your puppy's response to verbal cues.
- Introducing two new behaviors: "Leave It" and "Drop It".
- Providing a productive and safe outlet for your puppy's chewing.
- Getting your puppy comfortable with your presence by a valued resource like their food bowl.

BY THE END OF THIS WEEK YOUR PUPPY SHOULD:

- Have interacted with or seen 10 new people.
- Happily engage in play with other puppies.
- Settle easily with a chew toy when asked.
- Be relaxed and calm when you are standing at their food bowl while they eat.
- Only play-bite with a "softer" mouth and light bites.
- Go into their crate on their own to sleep or find comfort.
- Not use whining and barking as a tool to get your attention.
- Remain in a "Stay" behavior for no less than 10 seconds while you move 3-5 feet away.
- Understand the concept of a "Drop It" behavior by dropping toys when asked.
- Understand the concept of a "Leave It" behavior by not trying to grab food from your hand when asked.
- Start to "Sit" and "Down" after you say the verbal cue word but before you do the lure associated with the behavior.

WEEK 5 CURRICULUM
NOT EVEN THE
🐾 DRYWALL IS SAFE 🐾

10-MINUTE MORNING TRAINING SESSIONS

DAY 29	☐ Practice the "Recall": 10 repetitions ☐ Practice "Down": 15 repetitions
DAY 30	☐ Practice "Leave It": 10 repetitions ☐ Practice Leash Training
DAY 31	☐ Practice the "Recall": 10 repetitions ☐ Practice "Leave It": 10 repetitions
DAY 32	☐ Practice the "Recall": 10 repetitions ☐ Practice "Drop It": 10 repetitions
DAY 33	☐ Practice "Sit": 15 repetitions ☐ Practice the "Recall": 10 repetitions
DAY 34	☐ Practice "Leave It": 10 repetitions ☐ Practice "Stay": 10 repetitions
DAY 35	☐ Practice "Leave It": 10 repetitions ☐ Practice "Down": 15 repetitions

GAMES TO INCORPORATE INTO PLAYTIME THIS WEEK

"Tug of War" | "Red Light, Green Light"

10-MINUTE AFTERNOON TRAINING SESSIONS

DAY 29	☐ Practice "Drop It": 10 repetitions
DAY 30	☐ Practice "Sit": 15 repetitions ☐ Practice "Stay": 10 repetitions
DAY 31	☐ Practice "Stay": 10 repetitions ☐ Practice "Down": 15 repetitions
DAY 32	☐ Practice "Down": 15 repetitions ☐ Practice "Drop It": 10 repetitions
DAY 33	☐ Practice "Down": 15 repetitions ☐ Practice "Touch": 10 repetitions
DAY 34	☐ Practice "Sit": 15 repetitions ☐ Practice "Stay": 10 repetitions
DAY 35	☐ Practice "Down": 15 repetitions ☐ Practice "Touch": 10 repetitions

FIELD TRIPS

- [ ] Carry your puppy through a shopping center, store, or bank.
- [ ] Sit at a busy coffee shop with your puppy on your lap.

SOCIALIZATION

- [ ] Brush and groom your puppy.
- [ ] Perform a handling routine.
- [ ] Brush your puppy's teeth.
- [ ] Introduce your puppy to, or let them see, more men.
- [ ] Introduce your puppy to, or let them see, more women.
- [ ] Have your puppy play with other vaccinated puppies who play well.
- [ ] Expose your puppy to cars, cyclists, and runners.
- [ ] Expose your puppy to wheelchairs, walkers, canes and crutches.
- [ ] Take your puppy on an elevator ride.
- [ ] Play everyday sounds that will be a part of your puppy's life (traffic noises, babies crying, toddlers screaming, fireworks etc.) at a very low volume while they eat.

HELPFUL TIPS

- 🐾 Without chasing your puppy, slowly and calming retrieve anything they aren't supposed to chew on. Chasing becomes a game and will encourage them to chew on the item again.

- 🐾 Puppies learn to ignore verbal cue words that are repeated over and over. Say your cue word once to request a behavior, and if your puppy doesn't respond, lure them into the position instead.

- 🐾 "Tug-of-War" is a great way to teach your puppy to listen to cues and perform behaviors like "Sit" when they are excited or distracted.

- 🐾 Don't leave toys lying around. Unlimited access to toys gives a puppy a sense of entitlement, when instead they should consider toys a reward and privilege.

DEVELOPING GOOD DAILY HABITS

Habit	M	T	W	T	F	S	S
Ignore your puppy when they whine and bark for your attention.	☐	☐	☐	☐	☐	☐	☐
Stand by your puppy and drop treats in their bowl while they eat either breakfast or dinner.	☐	☐	☐	☐	☐	☐	☐
Periodically place a treat between your puppy's paws when they are calm and lying down.	☐	☐	☐	☐	☐	☐	☐
Ask your puppy to "Sit" before feeding them at breakfast and dinner.	☐	☐	☐	☐	☐	☐	☐
When you come home and your puppy greets you, wait for any jumping to stop and all four paws are on the ground before petting them.	☐	☐	☐	☐	☐	☐	☐
Say "OUCH" loudly and emphatically to hard play-bites. Praise and redirect your puppy's biting to a chew toy.	☐	☐	☐	☐	☐	☐	☐
Put your puppy in their crate, exercise pen, or puppy room for some alone time and refer to the isolation distress section for creating positive alone experiences.	☐	☐	☐	☐	☐	☐	☐

CHEWING

WHAT TYPE OF CHEWER IS YOUR PUPPY?

Your puppy has a hardwired desire to chew. As a puppy parent, your job is to set the boundaries on what is appropriate to chew. Your puppy will have a preferred chewing style that has implications for what chew toys are most appropriate and safest for them to use. Your puppy will likely fall into one of three chewing categories: inhaler, destroyer, or nibbler. Pay attention to your puppy's chewing style to figure out the best and safest toys to give them.

INHALER	*Your puppy bites off large chunks of edible chews (chew toys meant for consumption like Bully Sticks and Nylabones) and swallows them fast.*
DESTROYER	*Your puppy thoroughly destroys whatever they sink their teeth into. They may or may not swallow what they destroy.*
NIBBLER	*Your puppy takes their time to savor their chew toys.*

TYPES OF TOY FOR EACH CHEWER

INHALER	*Rubber Toys, Rope Toys, Stuffed Toys*
DESTROYER	*Rubber Toys, Edible Chews and Treats*
NIBBLER	*Rubber Toys, Rope Toys, Stuffed Toys, Edible Chews and Treats*

MORE ON THE DIFFERENT TYPES OF CHEW TOYS

RUBBER TOYS	*As long as they're the correct size for your puppy and aren't too flimsy, they represent one of the safest options.*
EDIBLE CHEWS & TREATS	*Short-lasting and high in calories, but they do offer some quick chewing relief and dental health. Throw these chews out when they're small enough to be swallowed.*
ROPE TOYS	*Always supervise your puppy with these toys. Pulled strands can lead to dangerous digestive obstructions.*
STUFFED TOYS	*Beware of poorly constructed or poor-quality stuffed toys; you don't want the fabric or filling to end up in your puppy's digestive tract.*

HELPFUL TIPS

🐾 Bored puppies will chew everything from drywall to couch cushions. Give your puppy plenty of fun and safe chew toys to keep their brain busy and their jaw occupied!

NOTES

LEAVE IT

WHY WE TEACH "LEAVE IT"

A "Leave It" behavior has your puppy ignore an object they find interesting. "Leave It" helps your puppy develop self-control and can keep your puppy safe.

HOW TO TEACH YOUR PUPPY "LEAVE IT"

STEP 1	*Show your puppy a treat and then enclose it in your hand by making a fist.*
STEP 2	*Say "Leave It". When your puppy stops sniffing or licking your hand and backs away slightly to look at you, say "Yes" and reward them with the treat.*
STEP 3	*After a number of repetitions, place a treat in an open palm without making a fist. Say "Leave It". If your puppy waits quietly or looks at you, say "Yes" and reward them with a treat. But if your puppy moves toward the treat, say "Nope" and close your hand into a fist and go back to practicing steps 1 and 2.*
STEP 4	*Once your puppy has mastered step 3, try placing the treat on the floor. Say "Leave It" and if your puppy obeys, say "Yes" and let them have the treat. If they go for the treat without waiting, say "Nope" and cover the treat with your hand and try again.*
STEP 5	*Put your puppy's leash on and place a treat on the floor. Walk your puppy slowly past the treat and say "Leave It"; if they walk past the treat without trying to grab it, say "Yes" and give them a treat. If they go for it, say "Nope" and try again or return to the previous step for more practice.*

VERBAL CUE WORD: "LEAVE IT"

TROUBLESHOOTING

🦴 If your puppy stops trying to get the treat but won't look at you and keeps their focus entirely on your hand, you can still reward them.

"LEAVE IT" PROGRESS

WEEK	PROGRESS
5	1 | 2 | 3 | 4 | 5
6	1 | 2 | 3 | 4 | 5
7	1 | 2 | 3 | 4 | 5
8	1 | 2 | 3 | 4 | 5

(1 = Learning, 5 = Perfected)

DROP IT

WHY WE TEACH "DROP IT"

Similar to "Leave It", "Drop It" helps keep your puppy safe and develops their self-control. Once this skill is mastered, you can easily get dangerous items away from your puppy without incident or potential aggression.

HOW TO TEACH YOUR PUPPY "DROP IT"

METHOD 1

STEP 1	Find a long toy and hold one end of it in your hand while your puppy bites down on the other end.
STEP 2	With your other hand, show your puppy a treat and say "Drop It".
STEP 3	As soon as your puppy drops the toy, say "Yes" and immediately feed them the treat.
STEP 4	Encourage your puppy to grab the toy again and continue practicing steps 1-3.
STEP 5	Now practice saying "Drop It" without a treat in hand. When your puppy drops the toy, continue to say "Yes" immediately. Repeat.

 VERBAL CUE WORD: "DROP IT"

METHOD 2

STEP 1   Let your puppy play with one of their favorite toys.

STEP 2   Watch them closely while the toy is in their mouth.

STEP 3   The moment your puppy drops the toy, say "Drop It" and "Yes". Reward your puppy with a treat.

STEP 4   Continue playing with your puppy and encourage them to pick up the toy so you can repeat steps 2 and 3.

STEP 5   After a number of repetitions, try saying "Drop It" before your puppy drops the toy on their own. If they respond, say "Yes" and reward them with a treat. If they don't, go back to steps 1-4 and re-attempt step 5 with more practice.

TROUBLESHOOTING

- If your puppy has no interest in the treat you are providing and would rather hold onto the toy, try a higher value reward like cooked chicken or cheese.

- If your puppy starts to tug on the toy after you say "Drop It", remain completely still and don't tug the toy back.

HELPFUL TIPS

- Once your puppy masters "Drop It", you can use it to keep them from biting or holding onto their leash.

"DROP IT" PROGRESS

WEEK	PROGRESS
5	1 | 2 | 3 | 4 | 5
6	1 | 2 | 3 | 4 | 5
7	1 | 2 | 3 | 4 | 5
8	1 | 2 | 3 | 4 | 5

(1 = Learning, 5 = Perfected)

🐾 GAMES 🐾
"TUG OF WAR"

"TUG-OF-WAR"

"Tug-of-War" is a game that has you tug on one end of an object while your puppy tugs and pulls on the other end with all their might.

WHY PLAY "TUG-OF-WAR"

"Tug-of-War" is a great way for your puppy to burn off excess energy, build confidence, and learn self-control.

STEP 1	*Presenting a tug toy to your puppy. Say "Take It" and, moving the toy back and forth, encourage your puppy to grab it.*
STEP 2	*With your puppy biting one end of the toy, gently begin to tug and pull on the other end. Verbally praise your puppy while you do this.*
STEP 3	*Pause the game and say "Drop It", prompting the behavior by placing a treat directly below your puppy's nose. When they drop the toy for the treat, say "Yes". Pick up the toy and repeat steps 1-3.*
STEP 4	*Once your puppy is familiar with the game try this variation to step 3 - after your puppy drops the toy, say "Sit" before you pick up the toy and continue playing. This helps build their self-control.*

TROUBLESHOOTING

🦴 If your puppy's imprecise attempts to bite lead to contact with your skin, end the game. Take the toy and walk away.

🦴 If your puppy refuses to drop the toy even with you staying completely still, you can either let your arm go limp until your puppy drops it or end the game for the day by walking away.

HELPFUL TIPS

🐾 Eventually your puppy will know to take the tug toy upon hearing you say "Take It" and there will be no need to move the toy back and forth.

🐾 When your puppy is reliably dropping the toy upon request, you no longer need to prompt them with a reward.

🐾 You should always be the one to initiate "Tug-of-War" with your puppy and decide when it ends. Between play sessions, put the tug toy away.

🐾 "Tug-of-War" is not appropriate for children as they will not be able to adequately control your puppy's excitement level.

GAMES
"RED LIGHT, GREEN LIGHT"

"RED LIGHT, GREEN LIGHT"

"Red Light, Green Light" is a game where your puppy has to listen for guidance on when to walk and when to sit.

WHY PLAY "RED LIGHT, GREEN LIGHT"

"Red Light, Green Light" is a great way to practice the "Sit" behavior, work on your puppy's self-control, and teach them to instinctively sit whenever you stop on a walk.

STEP 1	Have one person, the 'caller', stand to one side of the room.
STEP 2	At the opposite side of the room, put your puppy's leash on and hold it in one hand.
STEP 3	When the caller says "Green Light" – start walking with your puppy. When they say "Red Light" – come to a complete stop and ask your puppy to sit.
STEP 4	After a "Red Light", the caller will count to five out loud. Your puppy's job is to stay seated during that time. If they are unsuccessful, you and your puppy receive a penalty and must take five steps back.
STEP 5	If your puppy successfully sits during the "Red Light", say "Yes" and reward them with a treat.
STEP 6	When your puppy reaches the caller, the game is over and you're ready to start over!

MY PUPPY'S FAVORITE GAMES

WEEK SIX: GOOD HABITS LEAD TO BETTER RESULTS

INTRODUCTION

WHAT TO KNOW:
PREPARING FOR THE WEEK AHEAD

If you find yourself with more training time because your puppy has picked up on behaviors quickly, focus on playing games and reinforcing tasks highlighted in the "Developing Good Daily Habits" section of each week. Games are a great way to bond with your puppy and practice behaviors, and the recommendations found in the "Developing Good Daily Habits" section play an important preventative role when it comes to behavioral challenges.

TO-DO LIST

SECTIONS TO READ	DONE
No new sections to read this week!	☐

LEARNING OUTCOMES

The Focus of This Week Is On:

- Ensuring that the "Developing Good Daily Habits" tasks are making it into your normal routine.
- Strengthening the previously taught behaviors in preparation for increasingly difficult progressions that are on the way.
- Changing the conditions under which you normally ask your puppy to perform behaviors.

BY THE END OF THIS WEEK YOUR PUPPY SHOULD:

- *Have interacted with or seen 10 new people.*
- *Sit unprompted before receiving breakfast and dinner.*
- *Be able to observe a fast-moving subject like a car, cyclist or runner without barking or lunging.*
- *Reliably greet you without jumping by keeping four paws on the ground.*
- *Reliably perform a "Touch" behavior when you are across the room.*
- *Reliably perform a "Leave It" behavior when asked.*
- *Reliably perform a "Recall" behavior in a quiet training environment.*
- *Remain in a "Stay" behavior for no less than 20 seconds while you move 5-7 feet away.*
- *Perform a "Sit" and "Down" behavior in a quiet training environment without the aid of a lure.*

WEEK 6 CURRICULUM
GOOD HABITS LEAD TO
❖ BETTER RESULTS ❖

10-MINUTE MORNING TRAINING SESSIONS

DAY 36	☐ Practice "Sit" using only a verbal cue word (no lure): 15 repetitions ☐ Practice "Leave It": 10 repetitions
DAY 37	☐ Practice "Stay": 10 repetitions ☐ Practice "Leave It": 10 repetitions
DAY 38	☐ Practice "Down" using only a verbal cue word (no lure): 15 repetitions ☐ Practice "Touch": 10 repetitions
DAY 39	☐ Practice the "Recall": 10 repetitions ☐ Practice "Leave It": 10 repetitions
DAY 40	☐ Practice "Down" using only a verbal cue word (no lure): 15 repetitions ☐ Practice Leash Training
DAY 41	☐ Practice "Stay": 10 repetitions ☐ Practice "Drop It": 10 repetitions
DAY 42	☐ Practice "Stay": 10 repetitions

GAMES TO INCORPORATE INTO PLAYTIME THIS WEEK

"Tug of War" | "Red Light, Green Light"

10-MINUTE AFTERNOON TRAINING SESSIONS

DAY 36	☐ Practice "Down" using only a verbal cue word (no lure): 15 repetitions ☐ Practice the "Recall": 10 repetitions
DAY 37	☐ Practice "Stay": 10 repetitions ☐ Practice "Drop It": 10 repetitions
DAY 38	☐ Practice "Touch": 10 repetitions ☐ Practice "Drop It": 10 repetitions
DAY 39	☐ Practice "Drop It": 10 repetitions ☐ Practice "Leave It": 10 repetitions
DAY 40	☐ Practice "Sit" using only a verbal cue word (no lure): 15 repetitions ☐ Practice "Leave It": 10 repetitions
DAY 41	☐ Practice "Down" using only a verbal cue word (no lure): 15 repetitions ☐ Practice "Drop It": 10 repetitions
DAY 42	☐ Practice "Sit" using only a verbal cue word (no lure): 15 repetitions ☐ Practice "Leave It": 10 repetitions

FIELD TRIPS

- [ ] Sit at a busy coffee shop with your puppy on your lap.
- [ ] Take your puppy on a car ride.

SOCIALIZATION

- [ ] Grab your puppy's collar and release it.
- [ ] Brush and groom your puppy.
- [ ] Perform a handling routine.
- [ ] Brush your puppy's teeth.
- [ ] Introduce your puppy to, or let them see, more toddlers and young children.
- [ ] Have your puppy play with friendly, vaccinated, adult dogs.
- [ ] Expose your puppy to people riding skateboards and/or scooters.
- [ ] Expose your puppy to more cars, cyclists, and runners.
- [ ] Expose your puppy to any sports equipment commonly used in your household.
- [ ] Place or walk your puppy on more slippery, hard, and wet surfaces.

HELPFUL TIPS

- 🐾 Rotate chew toys in and out of play so your puppy doesn't get bored of them.
- 🐾 Puppies happily respond when called for something fun or yummy but are more reluctant if it means ending a play session or wrapping up a walk. Call them for mostly positive reasons and they will continue listening.

DEVELOPING GOOD DAILY HABITS

When you come home and your puppy greets you, ask for a "Sit" or "Touch" behavior before you pet them.

M | T | W | T | F | S | S
☐ ☐ ☐ ☐ ☐ ☐ ☐

While your puppy is eating at mealtime, pick up their bowl 1-2 feet off the ground and, while they watch, drop a treat in the bowl before placing it back on the ground.

M | T | W | T | F | S | S
☐ ☐ ☐ ☐ ☐ ☐ ☐

Restrict access to food and wipe up crumbs on counter tops.

M | T | W | T | F | S | S
☐ ☐ ☐ ☐ ☐ ☐ ☐

Have your puppy "Sit" before feeding them or allowing them to go outside.

M | T | W | T | F | S | S
☐ ☐ ☐ ☐ ☐ ☐ ☐

Don't leave toys lying around the house. Put them away when your puppy is done playing with them.

M | T | W | T | F | S | S
☐ ☐ ☐ ☐ ☐ ☐ ☐

Ask your puppy to "Wait" before letting them out of their crate.

M | T | W | T | F | S | S
☐ ☐ ☐ ☐ ☐ ☐ ☐

WEEK SEVEN: PROOFING MAKES PERFECT

INTRODUCTION

WHAT TO KNOW: PREPARING FOR THE WEEK AHEAD

At this stage your puppy has been exposed to many of the people and surroundings they will commonly encounter over the course of their lives. Reflect on your puppy's socialization experiences and consider which ones, if any, made your puppy uncomfortable. Repeat these interactions to give your puppy more opportunities to build their confidence so they don't become fearful, nervous or aggressive every time they find themselves in these situations. Keep it positive by having your puppy stay at a distance where they aren't showing any signs of distress and, as usual, bring lots of treats!

TO-DO LIST

SECTIONS TO READ	DONE
Proofing	☐
Evaluating Behaviors	☐
Games: "Hide and Go Seek" & "Guess Who"	☐

LEARNING OUTCOMES

The Focus of This Week Is On:

- Reflecting on the socialization experiences your puppy has had to date.
- Preparing to take the behavior evaluation tests for the "Sit", "Down", "Stay", and "Recall" behaviors.

BY THE END OF THIS WEEK YOUR PUPPY SHOULD:

- Have interacted with or seen 10 new people.
- Walk beside you with a loose leash around your backyard or home.
- Reliably respond to "Crate".
- Reliably perform a "Drop It" behavior when asked.
- Perform a "Sit" behavior for at least two of the test items on the behavior evaluation test.
- Perform a "Down" behavior for at least two of the test items on the behavior evaluation test.
- Perform a "Recall" behavior for at least two of the test items on the behavior evaluation test.
- Perform a "Stay" behavior for at least two of the test items on the behavior evaluation test.

WEEK 7 CURRICULUM PROOFING MAKES ❖ PERFECT ❖

10-MINUTE MORNING TRAINING SESSIONS

DAY 43	☐ Practice "Sit" using only a verbal cue word (no lure): 15 repetitions ☐ Practice "Down" using only a verbal cue word (no lure): 15 repetitions
DAY 44	☐ Practice "Stay": 10 repetitions ☐ Practice Leash Training
DAY 45	☐ Practice "Leave It": 10 repetitions ☐ Practice "Drop It": 10 repetitions
DAY 46	☐ Practice "Drop It": 10 repetitions
DAY 47	☐ Practice Leash Training
DAY 48	☐ Complete the behavior evaluation test for "Sit"
DAY 49	☐ Practice "Touch": 10 repetitions ☐ Practice "Leave It": 10 repetitions

GAMES TO INCORPORATE INTO PLAYTIME THIS WEEK

"Hide and Go Seek" | "Guess Who"

10-MINUTE AFTERNOON TRAINING SESSIONS

DAY 43	☐ Practice "Sit" and "Down" saying your verbal cue words while sitting in a chair: 5 repetitions each ☐ Practice "Sit" and "Down" saying your verbal cue words while raising your hands above your head: 5 repetitions each
DAY 44	☐ Have your puppy run by a pile of books on the floor while practicing the "Recall" behavior: 5 repetitions ☐ Walk in a circle around your puppy while they are performing a "Stay" behavior: 5 repetitions
DAY 45	☐ Place a book in front of your puppy while they are performing a "Stay" behavior: 5 repetitions ☐ Turn away from your puppy while they are performing a "Stay" behavior: 5 repetitions
DAY 46	☐ Have your puppy run by a treat on the floor while practicing the "Recall" behavior: 5 repetitions ☐ Practice "Sit" and "Down" saying your verbal cue words while you are turned away from your puppy: 5 repetitions each
DAY 47	☐ Complete the behavior evaluation test for "Stay"
DAY 48	☐ Complete the behavior evaluation test for "Down"
DAY 49	☐ Complete the behavior evaluation test for the "Recall"

FIELD TRIPS

- [ ] Take your puppy to a friend's house.

SOCIALIZATION

- [ ] Gently squeeze your puppy's paws and trim or dremel their nails (pretend if they don't need their nails trimmed).
- [ ] Bathe your puppy.
- [ ] Perform a handling routine.
- [ ] Introduce your puppy to, or let them see, people wearing hats, backpacks and sunglasses.
- [ ] Introduce your puppy to, or let them see, people in uniform.
- [ ] Introduce your puppy to, or let them see, teenagers.
- [ ] Let your puppy play with more friendly, vaccinated, adult dogs.
- [ ] Place your puppy on, or walk them through, snow and/or wet grass.
- [ ] Expose your puppy to balloons, street signs, and large garbage bins.
- [ ] Play everyday sounds that will be a part of your puppy's life (traffic noises, babies crying, toddlers screaming, fireworks etc.) at a very low volume while they eat.

HELPFUL TIPS

- 🐾 It's normal for your puppy's training to regress when you move to new locations or introduce new conditions. You are in competition with these distractions for your puppy's attention. Don't worry, with a little patience and a few repetitions your puppy will soon be back on track!

- 🐾 The best way to catch a puppy on the run is to get their attention, then walk or run in the opposite direction. Avoid chasing them, if possible.

DEVELOPING GOOD DAILY HABITS

	M	T	W	T	F	S	S
When you come home and your puppy greets you, ask them for a "Sit" or "Touch" behavior before you pet them.	☐	☐	☐	☐	☐	☐	☐
While your puppy is eating at mealtime, pick up their bowl 1-2 feet off the ground and, while they watch, drop a treat in the bowl before placing it back on the ground.	☐	☐	☐	☐	☐	☐	☐
Ask your puppy to "Wait" before letting them out of their crate.	☐	☐	☐	☐	☐	☐	☐
Have your puppy "Sit" before feeding them or allowing them to go outside.	☐	☐	☐	☐	☐	☐	☐
When your puppy plays with a toy, offer them a treat. When they drop the toy, take it away for a few moments before giving it back.	☐	☐	☐	☐	☐	☐	☐
Don't let your puppy on your furniture without permission.	☐	☐	☐	☐	☐	☐	☐
Periodically place a treat between your puppy's paws when they are calm and lying down.	☐	☐	☐	☐	☐	☐	☐

PROOFING

WHY WE PROOF BEHAVIORS

The final step in teaching a puppy any behavior involves getting your puppy to successfully perform the behavior under a variety of different conditions. This step is called proofing. When behaviors have been proofed, you can count on your training to work in real world situations.

Puppies are not able to generalize the way humans do. Your puppy may understand "Sit" when asked to perform the behavior where they learned it (e.g. at home), but they won't understand the request when the location changes or other contextual cues are different. For that reason, it's necessary to reteach each behavior under different conditions. Don't worry, the process to re-learn behaviors in a new context tends to be much quicker.

To illustrate with an example, when your parents told you not to put your elbows on the dinner table, you generalized this rule to include all dinner tables. For a puppy, that rule only applies to that specific table, when that same parent gives the instruction. Until the behavior is proofed, they won't understand that the rule applies all the time and at every table.

HOW TO PROOF A BEHAVIOR

STEP 1 — *Start by confirming that your puppy consistently performs behaviors in the place you first taught them.*

STEP 2 — *Now it's time to introduce new variables. For example, if you typically stand while training your puppy, try sitting down or wearing a hat and sunglasses. You can try any number of variations – get creative!*

STEP 3 — *Shift lessons to a new location with a few more distractions. This could be a new room in your house or somewhere outside. When your puppy is consistently performing behaviors here, progress to step 4.*

STEP 4 — *Move lessons yet again to another new location full of distractions.*

STEP 5 — *Continue practicing behaviors in different locations, under different conditions, with varying levels of distraction. When your puppy performs behaviors as reliably at a dog park as they do at home, you can consider those behaviors proofed.*

	# OF LOCATIONS TRAINED	PROOFED
SIT		☐
DOWN		☐
RECALL		☐
STAY		☐
LEAVE IT		☐
DROP IT		☐
TOUCH		☐

PROOFING FOR PUPPIES THAT AREN'T FULLY VACCINATED

Puppies who have not completed their series of vaccinations (typically those under 16 weeks) should hold off on proofing behaviors outdoors until they do so. Luckily, there are lots of fun ways to start proofing behaviors in your home and other indoor venues.

IDEAS FOR PROOFING UNVACCINATED PUPPIES

- Ask family members or close friends to train your puppy.
- Teach behaviors in different rooms in your home.
- Teach behaviors at a friend or family member's house.
- Teach behaviors while you have guests visiting.
- Teach behaviors in your backyard or garage.
- Face the opposite direction while having your puppy perform a behavior.
- Jump up and down while having your puppy perform a behavior.
- Place treats on the ground nearby while having your puppy perform a behavior.
- Ask a friend or family member to run past your puppy by while you have them perform a behavior

YOUR IDEAS

SIT	
DOWN	
RECALL	
STAY	
LEAVE IT	
DROP IT	
TOUCH	

EVALUATING BEHAVIORS

WHY WE EVALUATE BEHAVIORS

In order to know if your puppy is ready to progress training to new environments with more distractions, we test their current understanding of cue words in the original place they were taught with different variables.

SCORING

For each behavior, if a majority of checkmarks are in the "Yes" column, you are ready to start training that behavior in a location with more distractions.

TROUBLESHOOTING

- If your puppy doesn't respond to verbal cue words, it means they still rely on visual aids (lure) or simply need more practice. Remember to use your verbal cue words before you start luring. If you use the verbal cue while luring your puppy into a position, they will only pay attention to the lure.

DOES YOUR PUPPY RESPOND TO "DOWN" IF YOU SAY THE CUE WORD WHILE:

	YES	NO
RAISING YOUR HANDS OVER YOUR HEAD	☐	☐
SITTING IN A CHAIR	☐	☐
TURNING AWAY FROM THEM	☐	☐
JUMPING UP AND DOWN	☐	☐
WEARING A HAT AND SUNGLASSES	☐	☐

DOES YOUR PUPPY RESPOND TO "STAY" IF YOU SAY THE CUE WORD WHILE:

	YES	NO
SOMEONE RUNS PAST	☐	☐
PLACING A BOOK ON THE FLOOR IN FRONT OF THEM	☐	☐
WALKING IN A CIRCLE AROUND THEM	☐	☐
UNLOADING THE DISHWASHER	☐	☐
TURNING AWAY FROM THEM	☐	☐

DOES YOUR PUPPY RESPOND TO "SIT" IF YOU SAY THE CUE WORD WHILE:

	YES	NO
RAISING YOUR HANDS OVER YOUR HEAD	☐	☐
SITTING IN A CHAIR	☐	☐
TURNING AWAY FROM THEM	☐	☐
JUMPING UP AND DOWN	☐	☐
HIDING BEHIND A DOOR	☐	☐

DOES YOUR PUPPY COMPLETE A "RECALL" IF:

	YES	NO
THERE ARE OBSTACLES (E.G. BOOKS) ON THE GROUND	☐	☐
THEY HAVE TO RUN BY SOMEONE SITTING ON THE FLOOR	☐	☐
THEY HAVE TO RUN BY A TREAT LEFT ON THE FLOOR	☐	☐
THEY ARE BUSY CHEWING THEIR FAVORITE CHEW TOY	☐	☐
THEY ARE BUSY CHEWING A BONE	☐	☐

GAMES
"HIDE & GO SEEK" & "GUESS WHO"

"HIDE AND GO SEEK"

"Hide and Go Seek" is a game where your puppy races around your house to find the hidden players.

WHY PLAY "HIDE AND GO SEEK"

"Hide and Go Seek" is a great way to tap into your puppy's instincts to chase and find things while letting you practice the "Recall" behavior. This game will both mentally and physically tire your puppy out.

STEP 1	*In a group of 2-4 people, start by giving everyone a handful of treats.*
STEP 2	*One person asks your puppy to "Come" (or use your preferred "Recall" verbal cue) and feed them a few treats. In this time, the remaining players spread out to different hiding spots around the house.*
STEP 3	*Now, one at a time, the hidden player should take turns calling your puppy to "Come".*
STEP 4	*Once discovered, a player must feed your puppy treats.*

HELPFUL TIPS

- Decide in advance the order in which each person will call your puppy.
- Start with easy hiding spots and gradually increase the difficulty as your puppy gets the hang of the game.

"GUESS WHO"

"Guess Who" is a game where your puppy has to run to whoever's name is being called.

WHY PLAY "GUESS WHO"

"Guess Who" is a great way to practice the "Recall" behavior while teaching your puppy the names of family members and friends. It's also a game that larger groups can play.

STEP 1	*In a group of 3-5 people, start by giving everyone a handful of treats and sit together in a big circle.*
STEP 2	*Have one person ask your puppy "Where is [insert name of another person in the circle]?" Whoever was named would then tell your puppy to "Come".*
STEP 3	*If your puppy goes over to the right person, they earn a treat. If they approach the wrong person, everyone in the group should ignore the puppy and the named individual would repeat their call, saying "Come" until your puppy is successful.*
STEP 4	*The person who last offered the treat is now in charge of asking "Where is [insert name of another person in the circle]" and the game repeats. Continue until everyone in the circle has had a chance to call the puppy over.*

PUPPY TRAINING AND RAISING

WEEK EIGHT: THEY GROW UP SO FAST

INTRODUCTION

WHAT TO KNOW:
PREPARING FOR THE WEEK AHEAD

Get ready because you will soon have a teenager on your hands! Similar to human teenage years, your puppy will likely become more confident, independent, and rebellious. Rules will be tested and broken, boundaries pushed, and glimmers of maturity will start to appear. The time you've spent training, playing, and bonding with your puppy has put you in a great position to get through this more challenging stage with limited stress and frustration.

TO-DO LIST

SECTIONS TO READ	DONE
Loose Leash Walking	☐
Name Redirection	☐
8 Week Puppy Report Card	☐

LEARNING OUTCOMES

The Focus of This Week Is On:

- Building the foundation for loose leash walking outside.

- Evaluating your puppy's progress over the last 8 weeks.

BY THE END OF THIS WEEK YOUR PUPPY SHOULD:

- ⊘ Come back to your side when you stop walking because they've pulled on the leash.
- ⊘ Turn around and enthusiastically come back for a treat when asked during a walk.
- ⊘ Not be bothered when you pick up their bowl while they eat.
- ⊘ Have fewer than 5 bathroom related accidents per week.
- ⊘ Infrequently play-bite and generally use their mouths less while playing with a person.
- ⊘ Happily spend 30-40 minutes alone in their crate without whining and crying, even if you're home.
- ⊘ Happily exchange a favorite toy for treats.
- ⊘ Comfortably have their teeth brushed, paws squeezed, and nails trimmed or dremeled.
- ⊘ Calmly walk over different surface types.
- ⊘ Be comfortable with everyday objects ranging from strollers to garbage bins, etc.
- ⊘ Be comfortable hearing everyday noises ranging from traffic sounds and alarms, to sirens and fireworks.
- ⊘ Have been introduced or exposed to more than one hundred people.
- ⊘ Perform a "Recall", "Sit", "Down", and "Stay" behavior with increasing levels of distraction.

❋WEEK 8 CURRICULUM❋
THEY GROW UP SO FAST

This week includes outdoor activities in places that pose a higher risk to unvaccinated puppies. Complete this week's schedule only after your puppy has been fully vaccinated

10-MINUTE MORNING TRAINING SESSIONS

DAY 50	☐ Take your puppy on a walk: practice "Loose Leash Walking"
DAY 51	☐ Take your puppy on a walk: practice "Loose Leash Walking"
DAY 52	☐ Practice "Stay" outside while your puppy is on leash: 10 repetitions
DAY 53	☐ Practice "Name Redirection" while out for a walk: 5 repetitions
DAY 54	☐ Take your puppy on a walk: practice "Loose Leash Walking" ☐ Practice "Sit" while on a walk: 5 repetitions
DAY 55	☐ Practice "Name Redirection" while out for a walk: 5 repetitions
DAY 56	☐ Take your puppy on a walk: practice "Loose Leash Walking"

GAMES TO INCORPORATE INTO PLAYTIME THIS WEEK

"Hide and Go Seek" | "Guess Who" | "Red Light, Green Light" (play outside)

10-MINUTE AFTERNOON TRAINING SESSIONS

DAY 50	☐ Take your puppy on a walk: practice "Loose Leash Walking"
DAY 51	☐ Take your puppy on a walk: practice "Loose Leash Walking" ☐ Practice "Sit" during a walk: 5 repetitions
DAY 52	☐ Practice the "Recall" outside on a long line leash: 10 repetitions
DAY 53	☐ Practice the "Recall" outside on a long line leash: 10 repetitions
DAY 54	☐ Practice the "Recall" outside on a long line leash: 10 repetitions
DAY 55	☐ Take your puppy on a walk: practice "Loose Leash Walking" ☐ Practice "Stay" outside while your puppy is on leash: 10 repetitions
DAY 56	☐ Practice the "Recall" outside on a long line leash: 10 repetitions

FIELD TRIPS

- [ ] Take your puppy out for an evening walk.
- [ ] Take your puppy to an event that draws a crowd.
- [ ] Take your puppy on a trail walk.

SOCIALIZATION

- [ ] Brush your puppy's teeth.
- [ ] Perform a handling routine.
- [ ] Have your puppy play with friendly, vaccinated, adult dogs.
- [ ] Dress your puppy in any additional gear you'll expect them to wear: backpacks, booties, clothing, etc.
- [ ] Expose your puppy to outdoor garbage bins and signs.
- [ ] Introduce your puppy to, or let them see, more people of different ethnicities.
- [ ] Walk your puppy through a puddle of water.
- [ ] Place your puppy on, or walk them through, muddy surfaces and/or wet grass.
- [ ] Expose your puppy to automatic doors.
- [ ] Play everyday sounds that will be a part of your puppy's life (traffic noises, babies crying, toddlers screaming, fireworks etc.) at a very low volume while they eat.

HELPFUL TIPS

- 🐾 Find a quiet field or enclosed space like a tennis court when you are starting to train the "Recall" on a long line.

- 🐾 As your puppy becomes a teenager expect them to "forget" behaviors they previously mastered. Go back to the basics and repeat, when necessary.

- 🐾 Best to avoid dog parks until your puppy is at least 6 months old; until then they are likely to be overwhelmed.

- 🐾 Your puppy will go through a second "fear period" that usually lasts 3 weeks sometime between 6-12 months of age. To avoid your puppy developing any fear or aggression towards people, dogs or aspects of their environment they were previously comfortable with, you will need to continue to provide them with ongoing positive socialization experiences throughout the first year.

DEVELOPING GOOD DAILY HABITS

Habit	M	T	W	T	F	S	S
When your puppy plays with a toy, offer them a treat. When they drop the toy, take it away for a few moments before giving it back.	☐	☐	☐	☐	☐	☐	☐
While your puppy is eating at mealtime, pick up their bowl 1-2 feet off the ground and, while they watch, drop a treat in the bowl before placing it back on the ground.	☐	☐	☐	☐	☐	☐	☐
Ask your puppy to "Sit" before starting your walk.	☐	☐	☐	☐	☐	☐	☐
Speed up, slow down, and change directions while walking your puppy.	☐	☐	☐	☐	☐	☐	☐
Restrict access to food and wipe up crumbs on counter tops.	☐	☐	☐	☐	☐	☐	☐
Don't let your puppy on your furniture without permission.	☐	☐	☐	☐	☐	☐	☐
Ask your puppy to "Wait" before letting them out of their crate.	☐	☐	☐	☐	☐	☐	☐

LOOSE LEASH 🐾 WALKING 🐾

WHY WE TEACH "LOOSE LEASH WALKING"

"Loose Leash Walking" is a valuable skill that allows you to safely and comfortably walk your puppy outside. Once learned, you won't have to worry about being pulled off your feet whenever you leave the house. Your puppy will understand that by creating any tension in the leash, the walk stops.

HOW TO TEACH YOUR PUPPY "LOOSE LEASH WALKING"

STEP 1	*Make sure to bring lots of treats with you and let your puppy relieve themselves in their bathroom area before starting the walk.*
STEP 2	*Hold the end of the leash in one hand and use your free hand (the one closest to your puppy) to give your puppy treats while you walk. Feed your puppy treats down by your thigh every 5-10 steps and whenever your puppy looks up at you to check in. You can gradually increase the number of steps you take between giving your puppy treats.*
STEP 3	*Anytime your puppy starts pulling, stop walking. Wait until there is slack in the leash again and your puppy either looks at you or comes back toward you to say "Yes" and give them a treat.*
STEP 4	*Continue walking.*
STEP 5	*From time to time, stop walking and say "Sit". With your free hand, lure your puppy into a sit position. When they sit, say "Yes", reward them with a treat before resuming your walk.*

TROUBLESHOOTING

- If your puppy constantly pulls, keep them more engaged and focused by varying your walking speed and direction, and practicing "Name Redirection". The unpredictability is what keeps your puppy interested.

- If your puppy is not responding to "Name Redirection", try using the "Touch" behavior to redirect their attention back to you.

- If your puppy sits or lies down and refuses to walk, try either saying their name, "Come", "Touch" or making a noise. As soon as they get up to move, say "Yes" and give them a treat.

- If your puppy fixes their stare or barks at something, redirect their focus back to you right away and make a mental note of what caught their attention. Next time you're out for a walk, try to anticipate these distractions so you can redirect your puppy before it catches their attention.

HELPFUL TIPS

- Teaching your puppy to walk demands a lot of patience. Expect a lot of stop and go but, as long as you're consistently stopping anytime you sense any pulling, your puppy will soon follow your lead.

- Front attaching harnesses and gentle leaders provide greater control of a puppy's head, which is helpful for stronger breeds or puppies who pull enthusiastically.

- Avoid retractable leashes as they reinforce pulling behaviors in puppies. Keep your first few walks outside short and try to do them in a quiet area with fewer distractions.

"LOOSE LEASH WALKING" PROGRESS

PROGRESS

WALK 1	1 | 2 | 3 | 4 | 5
WALK 2	1 | 2 | 3 | 4 | 5
WALK 3	1 | 2 | 3 | 4 | 5
WALK 4	1 | 2 | 3 | 4 | 5
WALK 5	1 | 2 | 3 | 4 | 5
WALK 6	1 | 2 | 3 | 4 | 5
WALK 7	1 | 2 | 3 | 4 | 5
WALK 8	1 | 2 | 3 | 4 | 5
WALK 9	1 | 2 | 3 | 4 | 5
WALK 10	1 | 2 | 3 | 4 | 5
WALK 11	1 | 2 | 3 | 4 | 5
WALK 12	1 | 2 | 3 | 4 | 5
WALK 13	1 | 2 | 3 | 4 | 5
WALK 14	1 | 2 | 3 | 4 | 5

(1 = Learning, 5 = Perfected)

NOTES

NAME REDIRECTION

WHY WE TEACH "NAME REDIRECTION"

"Name Redirection" involves redirecting your puppy's focus back to you to prevent or stop undesirable behavior. A common situation to apply this skill is when your puppy pulls on their leash to see another dog, you would use name redirection to return their focus back to you.

HOW TO TEACH YOUR PUPPY "NAME REDIRECTION"

STEP 1	*When you're out for a walk, let your puppy walk past you while on the leash.*
STEP 2	*Once your puppy is in front of you, call their name and poke them on the back.*
STEP 3	*When they turn to look back at you, say "Yes", take a few steps back, and reward them with a treat.*
STEP 4	*Continue walking and keep practicing steps 1-3 at random intervals.*
STEP 5	*Your puppy will eventually turn around when they hear their name being called. When you reach this stage, you can stop giving them the physical poking cue.*

TROUBLESHOOTING

🦴 If your puppy barks and lunges toward other dogs, use "Name Redirection" or "Touch" when you see a dog approach. With your puppy focused on you, try to create more space for the other dog to pass or or keep your puppy distracted by feeding them treats.

"NAME REDIRECTION" WALKS

	NUMBER OF TIMES NAME REDIRECTION WAS USED	DID YOUR PUPPY'S FOCUS CHANGE?
WALK 1		Y | N
WALK 2		Y | N
WALK 3		Y | N
WALK 4		Y | N
WALK 5		Y | N

PUPPY REPORT CARD

TRAINING ACTIVITY	COMPLETED	PUPPY'S PROFICIENCY
HOUSETRAINING	Y | N	1 | 2 | 3 | 4 | 5
CRATE TRAINING	Y | N	1 | 2 | 3 | 4 | 5
ALONE TIME	Y | N	1 | 2 | 3 | 4 | 5
"MARK THE MOMENT"	Y | N	1 | 2 | 3 | 4 | 5
"NAME RECOGNITION"	Y | N	1 | 2 | 3 | 4 | 5
"NAME REDIRECTION"	Y | N	1 | 2 | 3 | 4 | 5
JUMPING UP	Y | N	1 | 2 | 3 | 4 | 5
PLAY-BITING	Y | N	1 | 2 | 3 | 4 | 5
CHEWING	Y | N	1 | 2 | 3 | 4 | 5
COMFORTABLE WITH PEOPLE NEAR FOOD BOWL	Y | N	1 | 2 | 3 | 4 | 5
NO WHINING OR BARKING FOR ATTENTION	Y | N	1 | 2 | 3 | 4 | 5
"RECALL" (INSIDE)	Y | N	1 | 2 | 3 | 4 | 5
"RECALL" (OUTSIDE)	Y | N	1 | 2 | 3 | 4 | 5
LEASH TRAINING	Y | N	1 | 2 | 3 | 4 | 5
LOOSE LEASH WALKING	Y | N	1 | 2 | 3 | 4 | 5
"LURED SIT"	Y | N	1 | 2 | 3 | 4 | 5
"LURED DOWN"	Y | N	1 | 2 | 3 | 4 | 5
"SIT"	Y | N	1 | 2 | 3 | 4 | 5
"DOWN"	Y | N	1 | 2 | 3 | 4 | 5
"STAY"	Y | N	1 | 2 | 3 | 4 | 5
"LEAVE IT"	Y | N	1 | 2 | 3 | 4 | 5
"DROP IT"	Y | N	1 | 2 | 3 | 4 | 5
"TOUCH"	Y | N	1 | 2 | 3 | 4 | 5

PUPPY TRAINING AND RAISING

SOCIALIZATION ACTIVITY	COMPLETED	PUPPY'S COMFORT RATING
INTERACTIONS WITH:		
MEN	Y | N	1 | 2 | 3 | 4 | 5
MEN WITH FACIAL HAIR	Y | N	1 | 2 | 3 | 4 | 5
WOMEN	Y | N	1 | 2 | 3 | 4 | 5
TODDLERS AND INFANTS	Y | N	1 | 2 | 3 | 4 | 5
YOUNG KIDS	Y | N	1 | 2 | 3 | 4 | 5
TEENAGERS	Y | N	1 | 2 | 3 | 4 | 5
ELDERLY	Y | N	1 | 2 | 3 | 4 | 5
PEOPLE OF DIFFERENT ETHNICITIES	Y | N	1 | 2 | 3 | 4 | 5
PEOPLE WITH DISABILITIES	Y | N	1 | 2 | 3 | 4 | 5
PEOPLE IN UNIFORM	Y | N	1 | 2 | 3 | 4 | 5
ADULT DOGS	Y | N	1 | 2 | 3 | 4 | 5
PUPPIES	Y | N	1 | 2 | 3 | 4 | 5
OTHER ANIMALS	Y | N	1 | 2 | 3 | 4 | 5
PEOPLE WEARING HATS AND/OR SUNGLASSES	Y | N	1 | 2 | 3 | 4 | 5
EXPERIENCE:		
WATCHING CARS, CYCLISTS AND RUNNERS	Y | N	1 | 2 | 3 | 4 | 5
COLLAR GRABS	Y | N	1 | 2 | 3 | 4 | 5
HANDLING ROUTINE	Y | N	1 | 2 | 3 | 4 | 5
BRUSHING TEETH	Y | N	1 | 2 | 3 | 4 | 5
GROOMING	Y | N	1 | 2 | 3 | 4 | 5
BATHING	Y | N	1 | 2 | 3 | 4 | 5
TRIMMING OR DREMELING NAILS	Y | N	1 | 2 | 3 | 4 | 5
HEARING CITY NOISES	Y | N	1 | 2 | 3 | 4 | 5
HEARING HOUSEHOLD NOISES	Y | N	1 | 2 | 3 | 4 | 5
EVERYDAY OBJECTS - UMBRELLAS, GARBAGE CANS, STROLLERS, ETC.	Y | N	1 | 2 | 3 | 4 | 5
WALKING ON SLIPPERY SURFACES	Y | N	1 | 2 | 3 | 4 | 5
WALKING ON HARD SURFACES	Y | N	1 | 2 | 3 | 4 | 5
WALKING ON WET AND MUDDY SURFACES	Y | N	1 | 2 | 3 | 4 | 5

CONGRATULATIONS

Finishing this puppy training and raising program is a major milestone - one that will surely set you and your puppy on a great path for many years to come! Over the last eight weeks you've experienced a number of puppy parenting firsts, and watched proudly as your puppy persevered through challenges. You've laid a great foundation for a well behaved puppy and should feel confident that you can and will tackle the demands of puppy adolescence with ease.

Continue to give your puppy consistency through structured daily routines, and revisit the lessons learned in this program when necessary. Be on the lookout for teachable moments in your daily interactions and, most importantly, continue to provide your puppy with positive socialization experiences. Most of all, enjoy the great adventures and memories that lay ahead for you and your new companion; there will be many!

BISCUIT

PUPPY TRAINING AND RAISING

EXTRAS

VACCINATION HISTORY

AGE	VACCINATION	DATE RECEIVED	
6-8 WEEKS	DHPP		☐
	Bordetella		☐
	Measles		☐
8-12 WEEKS	DHPP		☐
	Coronavirus		☐
	Leptospirosis		☐
	Bordetella		☐
	Lyme Disease		☐
12-24 WEEKS	Rabies		☐
14-16 WEEKS	DHPP		☐
	Coronavirus		☐
	Leptospirosis		☐
	Lyme Disease		☐
	Rabies		☐
12-16 MONTHS	DHPP		☐
	Coronavirus		☐
	Leptospirosis		☐
	Bordetella		☐
	Lyme Disease		☐

PUPPY TRAINING AND RAISING

AGE	VACCINATION	DATE RECEIVED	
ANNUAL	Coronavirus		☐
	Leptospirosis		☐
	Bordetella		☐
	Lyme Disease		☐
FIRST YEAR BOOSTER	DHPP		☐
EVERY 3 YEARS	DHPP		☐
EVERY 1-3 YEARS	Rabies (as required by law)		☐

❄ DEVELOPMENTAL ❄ TIMELINE

NEWBORN	❄ Sleepyhead phase.
WEEK 2	❄ Eyes open.
WEEK 3	❄ Tails start to wag, and puppies can sit or stand up. ❄ Ears open and the first teeth appear. ❄ Critical socialization period begins. ❄ Fear threshold is high and puppies aren't afraid to explore the world around them.
WEEK 4	❄ Walking, playing, and interacting with littermates.
WEEK 6	❄ Puppies start to eat food and are weaned off their mothers milk. ❄ DHPP vaccine given between week 6-8.
WEEK 8	❄ Fear emotion develops; everyday objects and experiences become more alarming. ❄ Ability to learn through training. ❄ Awake approximately 4-6 hours per day.
WEEK 9	❄ DHPP vaccine given between week 8-12.
WEEK 12	❄ Adult teeth start to come in; chewing increases dramatically over the next 3 months. ❄ Play-biting peaks. ❄ Most puppies drop down to three meals a day. ❄ Sleeping improves; puppies will sleep up to seven consecutive hours/night.
WEEK 14	❄ DHPP vaccine given between week 14-16. ❄ Puppies start needing regular daily exercise; roughly five minutes for every month of their age, up to twice a day. ❄ Critical socialization period ends.

WEEK 16	🐾 Puppies start to look like a smaller version of their adult self. 🐾 Puppies can be taken on short walks. 🐾 Puppies understand where they fit in the social order of the household.
MONTH 5	🐾 Puppies start to develop their adult coat. 🐾 Puppies will be less dependent on humans for security; assertiveness increases. 🐾 Puppies improve their bite inhibition and should not be play-biting their human family with intensity .
MONTH 6	🐾 Adolescent fear period begins anytime between 6-14 months of age and lasts 2-3 weeks. 🐾 Giant breeds have reached approximately half of their final weight. 🐾 Early stages of sexual development begin.
MONTH 8	🐾 Toy breeds have reached full size. 🐾 Teenage phase - dogs will intentionally "forget" a lot of the training they did as a puppy.
MONTH 12	🐾 Small and medium sized breeds have reached full size. 🐾 DHPP booster and rabies vaccine given. 🐾 1 year in a puppy's life is equivalent to 16 years of a human life; their maturity will reflect this.
YEAR 2	🐾 Large breeds have reached full size. 🐾 2 years in a puppy's life is equivalent to 24 years of a human life, their maturity will reflect this. 🐾 Many dog breeds will start to temper their energy and show stronger signs of maturity.

🐾 FIRSTS & FAVORITES 🐾

FIRSTS

ACCIDENT FREE WEEK: _____

LOST TOOTH: _____

BATH: _____

SWIM: _____

HAIRCUT: _____

FULL NIGHT'S REST: _____

LOOSE LEASH WALK: _____

SITS ON COMMAND: _____

DOWN ON COMMAND: _____

STAY ON COMMAND: _____

RECALL ON COMMAND: _____

LEAVE IT ON COMMAND: _____

DROP IT ON COMMAND: _____

TOUCH ON COMMAND: _____

PUPPY TRAINING AND RAISING

FAVORITES

FOODS: _____

TREATS: _____

PEOPLE: _____

SLEEPING SPOT: _____

ACTIVITIES: _____

GAMES: _____

FRIENDS: _____

TOYS: _____

PLACES: _____

MEMORABLE MOMENTS

MEMORABLE MOMENTS

QUESTIONS FOR MY TRAINER

QUESTIONS FOR MY TRAINER

QUESTIONS FOR MY VETERINARIAN

QUESTIONS FOR MY VETERINARIAN

CONTACT INFORMATION

VETERINARIAN CLINIC

EMERGENCY VETERINARY CLINIC

GROOMER

DOG WALKER

TRAINER

DOG SITTER

EMERGENCY CONTACT

NATIONAL PET POISON HELPLINE
1 (800) 213-6680

ASPCA POISON CONTROL HOTLINE
1 (888) 426-4435